Canadian History Through the Press Series

Confederation, 1854-1867

P. B. Waite

Canadian History Through the Press Series

General Editors:
David P. Gagan, Anthony W. Rasporich

Holt, Rinehart and Winston of Canada, Limited
Toronto: Montreal
Distributed in the United States of America by Mine Publications, Inc.

Editors' Preface

Newspapers are widely accepted by historians as useful vehicles of contemporary opinion. In a nation such as Canada, historically dependent on books and periodicals imported from Great Britain and the United States as the principal disseminators of informed opinion, the local daily or weekly newspaper has been almost the sole native medium of information and attitudes. And the proliferation of Canadian newspapers since the early decades of the nineteenth century has created for students of Canadian history a vast reservoir of opinion reflecting the political, social, cultural, linguistic, religious and sectional diversity of our country. The *Canadian History Through the Press* series is an attempt to tap this reservoir by reproducing a cross section of journalistic opinion on major issues, events and problems of the Canadian past.

Using the press as a vehicle for the study of history has already been done with some success in the French series, *Kiosk,* which examines public issues and popular culture in volumes ranging from the Dreyfus affair to French cinéma. *Canadian History Through the Press* is not quite so ambitious a venture; but it does aim to introduce the student to events which were compelling subjects of discussion for Canadians through the medium in which public discussion most frequently took place. At its best, the Canadian press is a rich source of historical controversy, providing the historian with a sense of the excitement and contentiousness of contemporary issues. Newspaper editors like William Lyon Mackenzie, George Brown, Henri Bourassa and George McCullagh were themselves often at the centre of the political stage or were, like J. W. Dafoe of the Winnipeg *Free Press,* Joseph Atkinson of the Toronto *Star* and Gérard Pelletier of *La Presse* pundits whose voices were carefully heeded by national and local politicians. This is merely one example of the power of the press; but whatever the subject — Confederation, the Quiet Revolution, social reform, foreign policy or pollution — the press has operated (in Marshall McLuhan's words) as a "corporate or collective image [that] demands deep participation."

As editors of *Canadian History Through the Press* we are committed to the idea that students should be introduced to the study of Canadian history through contemporary documents from the very outset. The newspaper is a familiar, and therefore comfortable medium for the novice historian. We have chosen to use it exclusively, fully aware of the limitations of the press as an historical source. When a prominent Canadian politician observed recently that his colleagues spent much of their time "quoting yesterday's newspaper" he was acknowledging the power of the press not merely to reflect, but to dictate opinion. And Will Rogers' caricature of the man who "only knew what he read in the paper" is an equally cogent reminder that newspapers should not be used exclusively as a weathercock of opinion. The student, then, must and inevitably will come to grips with both the limitations and the advantages of newspapers as sources of history. In this respect, our series is also aimed at introducing the student to one of the historians most crucial problems, that of discriminating between conflicting accounts and interpretations of historical events.

The volumes currently planned for the *Canadian History Through the Press* series embrace topics ranging from the War of 1812 to the Quiet Revolution of the 1960's, from economic history to religious issues. While it is not immediately possible, we hope that in time the series will eventually embrace an even wider spectrum of subjects which permit us to sample not merely the thrust, but the quality, of Canadian life.

Anthony W. Rasporich,
David P. Gagan,
October, 1971

Author's Preface

This little book is an attempt to put together a selection of newspaper comments on Confederation, between 1856 and 1867. I have already made an extended run at the period between 1864 and 1867 in *The Life and Times of Confederation, 1864-1867*, which the University of Toronto Press first published in 1962. They have kindly agreed to let me republish any extracts here. It is my intention, however, to avoid duplication, provided I can do so without sacrificing anything essential. The main difficulty in this book is that no one has yet made a comprehensive review of British North American newspapers for the period 1854 to 1863. There were about 250 newspapers, from Newfoundland to Vancouver Island; that kind of a survey may be impossible for one man to do well, except as the unremitting work of a decade. I have worked through all the Nova Scotia papers, some in New Brunswick, in Canada East, in Canada West, and in Newfoundland. So the selection for the period 1854-1863 is based not, as I would have liked, upon a vast cross section of the British North American press, but upon a rather haphazard selection of some of the more important ones.

Here I must acknowledge with gratitude the help of R. A. Hill, whose M. A. thesis for McGill in 1966, "The English-speaking Minority of Lower Canada, the Press and Federal Union, 1856-60," has saved me a great deal of time. His thoughtful work has provided insights which, with his permission, I have quoted or paraphrased in my introduction. Even more, his newspaper quotations have covered ground that I have not yet been able to cover myself, and which, with his agreement, I have used freely. I should also like to acknowledge the help of A. W. Rasporich, both for his critical comments on this book and for his stimulating Ph.D. thesis for the University of Manitoba, "The Development of Political and Social Ideas in the Province of Canada, 1848-58" (1970).

P.B.W.
Halifax, Nova Scotia
April, 1971

Peter B. Waite is Professor and Head of the Department of History at Dalhousie University, Nova Scotia.

David P. Gagan, general editor of the *Canadian History Through the Press Series,* is Assistant Professor of History at McMaster University, Hamilton, Ontario.

Anthony W. Rasporich, general editor of the *Canadian History Through the Press Series,* is currently Assistant Professor of History at the University of Calgary, Alberta.

Contents

CONFEDERATION 1854 - 1867

Introduction

Newspapers in mid-nineteenth century British North America were engines of opinion. They gave news, of course, but a glance at even one issue of any of them will usually show that editorial opinions on current politics were their *raison d'être*.

Newspapers of the time were almost invariably just four pages, that is, one large sheet folded once. On the front page was the masthead[1] with virtually a full page of advertisements below, though sometimes with parliamentary reports or a speech that had overflowed from the important inside pages. The back page, page 4, too, was advertising, which as a rule spilled over inside into page 3. Page 2, and part of page 3 were the inside heart of the paper that most people turned to first. The news was there, of course, gathered by telegraph, from other British North American newspapers, or from British, European, or American papers; the letters to the editor were there; and if the provincial parliament was in session, there was a synopsis of parliamentary debates, often quite comprehensive in the big dailies; and finally, most important of all, there were the editorials.

Editorials were what the paper stood for, and what this book is mainly concerned with. Editorials bore the stamp of the paper's political faith. Usually it was faith in a party. As the Belleville *Hastings Chronicle* put it,

> If he [an editor] edits a party organ he is expected to defend the principles of that party against all comers. . . . The doctrine that the King can do no wrong is amplified and extended to party government.[2]

But sometimes a newspaper's loyalty was to a group within, or even to a particular member of, a party. Politicians occasionally ran their own newspapers. They either wrote editorials themselves, or at least if they did not, they made sure the editor knew and reflected their opinions. George Brown is a famous example, though by the eighteen-sixties he was not always writing the *Globe* editorials. To write all the editorials of the *Globe*, every mortal day but Sunday, was simply more than one man could manage. Charles Tupper, whenever he was in Halifax, wrote editorials for the Halifax *British Colonist,* which came out three times a week (the general rule at the time), but he certainly did not write all of them, probably not even most of them.

Newspapers were thus an extension of parliamentary battles into a wider and less civilized battlefield. It was a battle waged all year round, week in and week out. Those who still believe the egregious error that Victorians were stuffy need only read a few of the selections below to discover that they were not. Newspapers were in fact written with an eye to their audience, and, like television at the present time, they excelled in distortion and misrepresentation. They were also pretty good at mudslinging. Of course some newspapers were far worse than others; newspapers wrote, after all, to suit the taste of their own constituency. But to capture any reading audience, whatever the content of editorials might be, newspapers had to be well written. Sloppy, turbid, incomprehensible prose simply condemned a newspaper to oblivion, the prospect of which tended to stimulate lively and forceful writing. In this respect, newspapers were not charitable to each other. Take the following, from the Toronto *Daily Colonist,* August 12, 1858:

A Supposed case of Sunstroke

A middle-aged man was yesterday picked up in King Street in a state of extreme exhaustion, supposed at first to be the effect of sunstroke. It was afterwards found, however, that the foolish man had attempted to read four columns of the [Toronto] *Atlas* editorial. . . .

If, at times, newspapers opted for the lurid in preference to the judicious that was perhaps a defect of virtues. It was generally recognized, however, that the greatest art in writing was then, as it still is, that of conveying a substantial and purposeful argument in a graceful and readable way, seasoned with metaphor, and salted with a strong sense of the literature of the language.

Newspaper offices were often busy places, and editorials, especially if they were morning dailies, were usually written at night, often dashed off with one eye on the clock, the other on the printer not infrequently waiting in the wings to put the editorial into type as soon as the editor had laid down his pen. This element of haste, still characteristic of newspaper writing, has to be remembered before too much weight is given to what newspapers said. There is an instructive remark from the editor of the Hamilton *Spectator* to Sir John A. Macdonald in the eighteen-eighties. The editor had been chided by Macdonald for his virulent anti-Catholic editorials. He apologized to Macdonald, admitted that his language had been too strong, that "his articles were dashed off at night in haste without being revised, and that frequently he has had course to regret the severity of their tone when he and they had time to cool." But, the editor added, he was a Protestant, and the Hamilton *Spectator* was written to suit the taste of its Protestant subscribers.[3]

This suggests a further point. Newspapers, however much they may be considered engines of opinion, could not make or break public opinion; they could only shape it and direct it, and there were real limits on how much they could do. The editor of the *Globe* in the eighteen-eighties admitted that the moderate position it had taken in the Riel affair had lost the paper many subscribers. The *Unionist & Halifax Journal* published a steady stream of editorials urging Confederation, three times a week for three years, 1865 to 1867; but it does not follow that all its readers favoured Confederation. The *Unionist* was probably heavily subsidized; and it would be interesting to know just what was its real circulation and readership. It is also virtually impossible to find out.

The extent to which newspapers actually influenced the outcome of Confederation, the extent to which their advocacy altered opinions or drew waverers into supporting Confederation, is, of course, impossible to know. Though newspapers could not manufacture opinion they could make known what was previously unknown, clarify what was unclear. This last was a role of some importance in the Atlantic colonies, where Confederation really came in 1864 as something of a bombshell. Confederation had been talked of in the past, of course, but as something in the distance, an horizon that had not yet been reached. In 1864 Confederation was right in front of the Atlantic colonies, to be decided upon virtually at once. Newspapers could, and did, make known the form and content of Confederation, as well as advancing arguments for or against it.

Newspapers tended to be in advance of public opinion, especially in Newfoundland and in Nova Scotia, in supporting Confederation. They were much more conscious than their outport readers of the dimensions and scope a united British North America might have, and at the same time felt the limits of narrow colonial jurisdictions rather more.

In the late eighteen-fifties, in British North America there were about 285 newspapers issued, either weekly or more often, and this figure was to increase to about 380 by 1865. Of these 285, some 200 were in the Province of Canada, that is about one newspaper for every 10,000 people, a proportion roughly accurate for the Atlantic colonies. There were probably too many, if subscriptions be considered as the key to newspaper balance sheets. Saint John, New Brunswick alone had 13 newspapers for its population of about 40,000. New Brunswick as a whole had 24 newspapers for its population of 200,000. In the Atlantic provinces newspapers were helped by the prevalence of free postage for their dissemination; but even so, all British North American newspapers needed more than subscriptions to sustain them. Patronage of one kind or another was nearly indispensable. R. A. Hill sets this out in some detail for the eighteen-fifties and sixties. It is clear that in many cases government patronage meant the difference between profit and no profit, in some, between profit and loss. Some government printing and stationery orders did go to opposition presses, but every Government believed it had to reward its supporters and reward them as handsomely as possible. Devoted friends clearly expected return for their devotion. No newspaper gave its support for nothing. "Do these men serve the Government for Nought?" asked the Montreal *Weekly Herald*, May 14, 1859. The question was clearly ironic.

It is thus clear that one has to be circumspect, even cautious, with newspapers. As primary sources for history they are immensely valuable, and be it added, tremendous fun; but they clearly supported their "friends," and they thrived on excitement. When excitement was lacking, they would if they could manufacture some. The even tenor of people's lives, the real character of the society in which British North Americans, in the several colonies, lived, has to be read between the lines, in the advertisements, in the letters. The quiet life, which is most people's much of the time, has never been fairly dealt with by newspapers, and probably never can be. The business of newspapers was news, and comment on the news. What is news is quite different from what is living. History itself partakes heavily of this bias. Economic history, business history, social history promise to correct something of that difficult, inherent, perhaps unfortunate, habit of history of dealing mainly with the spectacular.

Besides the ordinary distortions attendant upon the vicissitudes of news-gathering, there was the simple fact that newspapers could print almost anything they pleased. Of course they were subject to the law of libel, but libel law had in the eighteen-fifties and sixties, and afterwards, a conspicuously high level of tolerance. Readers liked their newspapers lively; they still do. Altogether, historians who read newspapers one hundred years after they were printed have to remember they are not always dealing with pure raw material, but usually a selected and often a tendentious form of it. Newspapers may be telling the truth; they may be telling part of the truth; they may be saying what they wish were the truth; but they may also be saying nothing of substance at all.

*   *   *

The lines of argument suggested in this introduction are, perforce, tentative. There was discussion of Confederation in nearly all the colonies, in one form or another, both before Lord Durham's Report of 1839, and afterwards. This discussion was sporadic, but increased in volume and range as time went on. It increased sharply at particular times, 1848-9, 1857-9, and was to appear in its most intense form between 1864 and 1867. The Confederation movement, broadly speaking, grew stronger all the time, but there were sharp ups and downs imposed on top of this general movement. There are reasons for this pattern. Mainly the reasons are pressing economic or political ills, the latter often being an outgrowth of the former.[5]

The history of Confederation from 1863 to 1867 is by now fairly well established; the history is not so clear from 1856, when the issue first appears on the horizon of practical politics. In each of the British North American colonies Confederation appeared, and developed, for different reasons, and at a different pace. It appears in Newfoundland almost full-blown at the end of 1864. Interest by Newfoundland in the mainland colonies had begun in 1857 as the result of their support in Newfoundland's difficulties with the French shore. Newfoundland was also, significantly, the only colony to reply favourably to the initiative of the Province of Canada in 1858. The economic difficulties of the early eighteen-sixties were to emphasize Confederation as a haven of refuge at a difficult time.

In Prince Edward Island the possibility of union with the mainland provinces had often appeared as a threat emanating from London, or from the governors of Nova Scotia or New Brunswick. That threat was in terms of a forced legislative union with Nova Scotia or New Brunswick, exactly what had happened to the Colony of Cape Breton in 1820, when it was wholly merged with Nova Scotia, or what was to happen to Vancouver Island and British Columbia in 1866. Federal union of British North America posed different issues for Prince Edward Island, and broadly speaking it was, as far as Islanders were concerned, the only kind of union they would even consider. Basically, however, they wanted to be left alone, to deal with Downing Street in their own, rather intractable, fashion.

In Nova Scotia talk of Confederation in the eighteen-fifties developed partly from the difficulties of party government. Some disillusionment with responsible government is discernible in Nova Scotia in the eighteen-fifties and it produced a search for a less constricting way of realizing Nova Scotian aspirations. There were three main forms: some new formula for orientation of Nova Scotia within the British Empire; Confederation of British North America; or an economic union based upon an intercolonial railway from Halifax, through New Brunswick to Quebec City.

In New Brunswick there was less preoccupation with political ailments. Successive governors certainly thought that political life in New Brunswick was rather seamy, but that was not a universal opinion among New Brunswickers. In New Brunswick talk of British North American union was almost wholly the result of interest in a railway to Quebec, and the hopes for a customs union. The feeling was widespread that the railway and a common tariff was a necessity, and that if federal union was an inevitable concomitant of that, it too would be considered. The events from 1861 to 1867 show clearly that this preoccupation with an intercolonial railway continued to exist.

In the Maritime provinces generally, there had been discussion of British North American union in the eighteen-fifties; but it was discussion without the driving force behind it of any immediate practical problem. It thus seemed to the public devoid of any apparent, immediate, practical consequences. In the Atlantic colonies Confederation solved no pressing issues, except perhaps the Intercolonial Railway, and it was not central even to that. Only insistence by Nova Scotia and New Brunswick on the Intercolonial as an indispensable condition of Confederation made it part of the terms of union in 1867. The Intercolonial Railway was, in other words, the only practical form of Maritime interest in Confederation in the eighteen-fifties and early eighteen-sixties.

In the Province of Canada Confederation represented something wholly different. Confederation there was a specific solution for specific ills in the Province. Federation of the Province of Canada was a major issue in the late eighteen-fifties, that is, with Canada East and Canada West as two parts of a constituent and federal Province of Canada. This was the basis for the resolutions passed at the great Reform convention of 1859. Federation on this basis would relieve the tensions created by Canada East and Canada West having to share the same legislature. It would give them, so to speak, separate rooms, which they could furnish to their own taste, style, and expense. They would still eat together, use the same house, and even use the same roads, carriages, and horses. In other words, a central government of the Province of Canada would represent the continued identity of the interests of both sections in trade, and in the St. Lawrence canals, their essential interrelation, of which the Grand Trunk was the newest symbol. However, the Conservative party had not accepted federation of the Province of Canada; they took the view that the legislative union of 1841, with its quasi-federal devices in the administration of education and of civil law, was still viable; and when they finally did accept federation, in 1864, they took it in its wider, British North American context, called "Con"-federation. Confederation was for the Conservative party what federation had been for the Reform party, that is, a solution for the inherent difficulties of governing the Province of Canada.

These difficulties are well-known. Representation by population was not itself the main problem: rather it was an answer to other problems. Canada West became increasingly reluctant to accept legislation of matters vitally important to it, education, for example, that had been passed by a majority that was not itself from Canada West. Nor could Canada West easily accept the fact that the revenue of the Province of Canada should be spent upon projects of local interest to Canada East. Of this revenue Canada West contributed at least 60 percent, probably more. Had there been identity of interests between the two sections no objection would have been made; but there was not. There was only a vague consciousness of their economic interdependence.

Confederation in the Province of Canada was, thus, to have quite a different significance than in the Atlantic provinces. Canada West was to see it as a great measure designed to relieve the political grievances that had plagued the province from 1854 to 1864. Since Canada West had been the most annoyed by these grievances, it followed that Canada West was the most enthusiastic about Confederation. Canada East, however, had by the 1850's come to resist all attempts to change the constitution, and was thus clearly much more uneasy about Confederation. Altogether, however, with English Protestants in Canada East joining with Canada West in feeling the time had come for a change, the Province of Canada was to be a far more purposive and effective driving force for Confederation than any of the Atlantic provinces could be.

None of this, however, was clear in the late eighteen-fifties. There was just a chronic, and growing, sense of grievance over many issues. All issues were focussed effectively on one solution: representation by population. "Représentation basée sur la population" had first appeared from the French-Canadian side of the Assembly, for it was the French Canadians who at first were under-represented by the equality of Canada East and Canada West in the Canadian legislature. Papineau had himself introduced it in 1849. In Canada West, the Clear Grits had taken it up from about 1850 onward, mainly because any redistribution of seats would improve their standing in the fast-growing farming areas of the peninsula. After the 1851 census, however, actual preponderance of Canada West's population was confirmed. (952,000 to 890,000.) In 1853 George Brown, newly elected independent from Kent County, brought in a motion for "representation by population," only to have it resoundingly defeated by French Canadians and their allies in the Reform party.

By 1855, the French Canadians had switched their allegiance to the Conservatives, and were still in power. A separate school bill for Canada West came up in 1855, and was pushed through, late in the session, by this coalition, when many representatives from Canada West had already left Quebec to go home, in fact, by a majority essentially Lower-Canadian. To the anger of Canada West over this was added, in 1856, the hatreds engendered by the Corrigan case. Corrigan was an Irish Protestant who was beaten to death by Irish Catholics in Canada East. All seven assailants were acquitted by a Roman Catholic jury. Both issues came up in an Assembly that in

1856 was "spoiling for trouble."[6] Brown urged "representation by population" in the debate on the double majority, and summed up the problem as well as anyone on June 3, 1856.

> Mr. BROWN: . . . You must either maintain the Union [by adopting rep. by pop.] or dissolve it.
>
> Mr. DUFRESNE[7]: Dissolve it!
>
> Mr. BROWN: The hon. gentleman says, Dissolve it! That is precisely the point I have been endeavouring to put ever since I had a seat in this house. We have two countries, two languages, two religions, two habits of thought and action, and the question is can you possibly carry on the government of both with one Legislature and one executive? That is the question to be solved.[8]

By this time the *Globe's* systematic agitation for representation by population was already under way.

Then the Northwest question arose. In 1855 the last block of wild land in the western peninsula of the province was auctioned, and in the same year the Northern Railway opened through Barrie to Collingwood on Georgian Bay. The House of Commons in London had already determined upon a Select Committee to inquire into the renewal of the Hudson's Bay Company licence to trade, as well as into its role as owners and administrators of the colonies of Rupert's Land and Vancouver's Island. This great inquiry expanded the horizons and the ambitions of Canada West. On December 15, 1856, eighteen Reform MP's and some thirty-two newspaper editors called for the annexation of the territory of the Hudson's Bay Company to the Province of Canada. Three weeks later, in Toronto, there was a Convention of the Reform party that emphasized the same policy, as it emphasized also "representation by population." By now this vast debate over the future of the province, its difficulties, its hopes, its ambitions, had started in the newspapers.

*   *   *   *

The Confederation agitation of the later eighteen-fifties and its several ramifications has yet to be fully essayed. The bits and pieces that appear in the biographies of Brown, Macdonald, Galt, Cartier, and others are necessarily superficial, and they fail to tell anything like the full story of the considerable and wide-ranging discussion, in Parliament and press, of the political problems and the political solutions that lay before the province. By 1864, however, the Canadian public was sufficiently familiar with the possibilities of the various alternatives that when the Confederation proposal of June, 1864, came, its main principle was understood and rapidly accepted. To this understanding, the discussion of the later fifties made an immense, perhaps indispensable, contribution. It was, in fact, the absence of a similar debate in Nova Scotia and New Brunswick that goes far to explain the long uphill fight Confederation had in both colonies in 1864 and after. Thus Confederation was not to have in the Maritime colonies the driving force that it would have in the Province of Canada.

The debate in Canada centred on the question of the dissolution of the Canadian union or upon methods of its preservation. Dissolution was simple. The preservation of the Canadian union could take five forms:

1. The *status quo,* which, broadly speaking, the Conservative party with its strong French-Canadian constituency felt most at home with;
2. Representation by population;
3. The double majority principle, where legislation directly affecting either of the two sections of the province would be passed only by a majority of the members of that section;
4. Federation of the British North American colonies, of which federation of the Province of Canada would be an inevitable concomitant;
5. Federation of the Province of Canada alone, breaking it into two, or even three or more sections.

These five forms, and of course outright dissolution of the union, were continuously before Parliament and public during the later fifties. French Canadians found it difficult, if not impossible to accept representation by population, and they provided the strong bulk of support behind the Conservative party's attempts to preserve the status quo. Rather than representation by population French-Canadian Conservatives would even consider a form of federation, or, preferably, the double majority principle, as *La Minerve* of Montreal did in 1857, and as Joseph Cauchon, of *Le Journal de Québec* did in the Assembly in 1858.[9] Even dissolution of the Union was better than "rep. by pop."

The Rouges, on the other hand, were in a peculiarly difficult position. They found it difficult to accept Brown's representation by population, yet, if they had any hope of office they had to make some concessions. A. A. Dorion, the Rouge leader, admitted, on April 24, 1856, the justice of Canada West's position. He admitted Canada West had more people than Canada East — he guessed about half a million more, when it was actually less than half of that. He admitted that representation by population was a reasonable request. He insisted, however, that a federal union of the Province of Canada was a more realistic solution, and his preference was clearly for federation of the province. Failing that, however, he would support Brown. This probably was his position, too, in July, 1858 when he and Brown formed their celebrated three-day government. In other words, as a Liberal A. A. Dorion could agree with Brown: as a French Canadian he could not.[10]

The English Protestants of Lower Canada, whose political and economic power hardly needs emphasis, were, most of them, afraid of dissolution of the Union. Dissolution would, or at least could, destroy their economy, based upon the communication and, to a degree, dominance of the Upper-Canadian market; still more, dissolution would put them under the control of a French-Canadian majority in Lower Canada, precisely where they had been before 1841. They were equally unhappy with the prospect of a federation of the Province of Canada, unless the constitutional power of a future province of Lower Canada were well under the control of some federal power. Any substantial sovereignty for a province of Lower Canada was anathema to the English Protestants. Consequently most of them preferred the lesser danger, as it seemed to them, of alliance with French-Canadian Conservatives, in the hope of keeping the Union as it was. This was at least part of the basis of the Conservative party in Canada East. Thus, for quite different reasons, French Canadians and most English Protestants in Lower Canada were opposed to federation of the province, certainly the kind of decentralized federation that seemed to be in the minds of the Reformers and Rouges.

Confederation had been discussed by some French-Canadian writers, notably J. C. Taché in the Quebec *Courrier du Canada* in 1857, and Joseph Cauchon in *Le Journal de Québec* in 1858. They conceived of Confederation as a rather decentralized system of federal government, analogous to that of the United States. It seems to have appealed to these French-Canadian writers as a neat and systematic rationalization of existing political difficulties. It would, of course, also re-establish a provincial capital at Quebec, and it may be that this partly explains why newspaper projects for Confederation emanated from Quebec rather than from Montreal.

Some English-Canadian newspapers talked of Confederation also, such as the Montreal *Gazette,* a paper not far away from elements in the Conservative party. This is where A. T. Galt fits in. Galt, it must be remembered, was until 1858 one of the group of Lower-Canadian English Liberals, many of whom were often unhappy with Brown, as Dorion often was. Galt had, however, been moving to the right as his Grand Trunk connections continued to ramify, and as his large and growing family (three sons and eight daughters) suggested the increasing necessity of greater income. Galt was already an independent by early 1858. When he proposed the federation of British North America to the Canadian Parliament in July, 1858 he was not really the member of any party.

Galt's motion for a British North American Confederation and the debate upon it, is most interesting; but as much as it has been widely discussed since, it aroused no great interest at the time. It was too visionary and too far away; it did not cut closely enough to home. It was clear, though, that Galt's project had already some support outside Parliament, notably from the Montreal *Gazette*; but it is evidence of how little either Government or opposition were interested in such wide-ranging schemes that no debate worth mentioning was aroused by it in Parliament, and newspapers did not actively take it up. "Half a continent is ours," Galt had said, "if we do not keep quarrelling about petty matters and lose sight of what interests us most."[11] But petty matters were still the bread and butter of politics, and big solutions for the Canadian problem were still, for most politicians, in the empyrean.[12]

It is significant, however, that Galt was the man whom Governor-General Head sent for, when the Brown-Dorion government collapsed in August, 1858. That may reflect Head's interest in Confederation. Galt failed to form a government; but he did join the Conservative government that was formed under Cartier, and he brought his scheme for British North American federation with him. This did not, in the eyes of many, count for much. It was thought of by Liberals and Reformers as nothing much but a Conservative trick to pull in support, and which it probably was, however sincere Galt may have been. No Reformer could consider British North American federation with anything but partisan venom after the awful iniquity as it seemed to them, of the double shuffle of August, 1858.

As it turned out, Galt's Confederation proposals of 1858 failed to win any substantial support from the other "denizens," as one newspaper put it, of British North America, in the Atlantic Colonies.[13] A Canadian Minute of Council inviting discussion of British North American federal union, and requesting Colonial Office authorization of such discussion, was approved by the Governor-General on September 9, 1858, and duly forwarded to the other colonies and to London.[14] To the Atlantic colonies also went a covering letter, indicating that for the moment, until the Colonial Office had authorized discussion, the Canadian proposal was a matter mainly of information. New Brunswick replied that same month, September, 1858, suggesting that she was more interested in Maritime Union. Other provinces answered only after a Colonial Office dispatch, November 26, 1858, had declined to authorize such a meeting unless the provinces themselves asked for it.

Nova Scotia then agreed simply to lay the dispatches before the legislature. The truth was that Lord Mulgrave, the Lieutenant-Governor was hostile to the idea.[15] Prince Edward Island replied through its Lieutenant-Governor that though opinion generally was favourable, the Council had no settled views. Newfoundland indicated that she would attend any conference, but that proposals would have to have some tangible form before Newfoundland would be willing to take up "this very important question."[16]

Although Canadian initiative was renewed by Galt in 1859 with proposals for an intercolonial railway as well as a customs union, the trend in the Maritime colonies was toward Maritime union, and in Canada the Reform convention of November 1859 turned toward the federation of the Canadas.

What had happened to the Canadian Confederation initiative of 1858? It had arisen out of Canadian political grievances, and Conservative political frustrations. The basic grievances remained unsolved, but the new Cartier-Macdonald government had largely solved the frustrations, for the time being at least. It has to be admitted that the Confederation issue had some real advantages for the Cartier-Macdonald government. Confederation offered, in 1858, a convenient red herring for the Reform pack hot in pursuit of Macdonald over the double shuffle. Confederation promised also a solution for the political difficulties of Canada, without committing the government very far. It could be dropped when the Maritime colonies, or the Colonial Office, or both as it turned out, did not take it up. Confederation was, in other words, both harmless and useful. But another reason ought to be considered for the failure of the Confederation impulse in 1859: the ending of the depression of 1857-59. The New York stock market crash had come in 1857. Canada was affected as always she would be, by economic diseases below the border. There is a saying that when the United States gets a cold, Canada starts to sneeze. Agitation for great political changes is a certain sign that all is not well somewhere, and rarely is the illness simply confined to politics. The talk of federation in 1849 was the obverse of the annexation movement of 1849, and both came from the economic vicissitudes of 1847-49. The Rebellion Losses Bill of 1849 had merely set it all off. It was to be so, too, with the Confederation movement of 1864-67. There was then no depression, but there was the prospect of the end of the Reciprocity Treaty, discussion of which started seriously in Congress in May, 1864. Thus the economic depression 1857-59 stimulated discussion of political change. Equally, when the depression lifted, discussion tended to die down.

Another reason for the failure of the 1858 initiative was the cool reception the proposals received in London. W. L. Morton, in *The Critical Years,* lays most of the blame upon the Colonial Office. That may not be quite just; but it is conspicuous that Confederation succeeded after 1864 when it had the positive, indeed the ruthless backing of the Colonial Office; the movement failed in 1858-59 when it did not get it. The Colonial Office would probably have accepted Confederation even in 1858 or 1859 had it been roundly supported by the colonies themselves. But it was not. So the Colonial Office could, and did, sit quietly and do nothing.

In the session of 1860 the Canadian legislature met at Quebec, the first time it had met there since 1855. It was to stay there until the move to the new capital, already chosen at Ottawa, which was to take place at the end of 1865. On the first day of that 1860 session Brown gave notice of motion that the Reform party would propose federation of the Province of Canada, which had been agreed to at the Reform convention at Toronto in November, 1859.

Brown introduced his motion on April 30, 1860. But even before debate started it was already clear that the agreement of Reformers about a future constitution for the province was more apparent than real. The debates of 1860 only sharpened the divisions within the Reform party over a constitutional program. When the vote came on the first of Brown's resolutions, on dissolution of the Union preparatory to its federation, it was defeated 66 to 27. Brown's motion for a federation of the province was defeated 74 to 32. The result of the vote profoundly discouraged Brown, and it weakened not only the Reform party but the project of the federation of the province.[17] At the same time it strengthened the Conservative party, and that vague project that the Conservative government had talked about in 1858 and 1859, but did not yet really believe in, Confederation of all the North American colonies.

Yet for the moment even the broader union suggested by Confederation seemed snared in the manifold provincialism of disparate and separated colonies. After the outbreak of the American Civil War in 1861, and the Trent crisis of November, 1861, events combined to stress military and logistical issues, both exemplified in the active negotiations for the Intercolonial Railway in 1861 and 1862. The defeat of the Cartier Conservative government in 1862 over a militia bill brought to power a Reform government, without George Brown, seeking to manage the problems of the Province of Canada by compromises and a half-hearted attempt to resurrect the double majority principle. It narrowly staved off defeat several times, but finally broke down in April, 1864. The collapse, in June, 1864, of the Conservative government that followed, opened the way to the negotiations that produced the great coalition and its sponsoring of Confederation.

Notes to Introduction

1. The masthead of the newspapers is italicized throughout this book, e.g., Quebec *Le Canadien*, Halifax *Acadian Recorder*, or *Yarmouth Tribune*, whatever the masthead actually was.

2. Belleville *Hastings Chronicle*, August 29, 1866. This newspaper was the Reform party's standard-bearer in Belleville. The Conservative rival was Mackenzie Bowell's *Intelligencer*.

3. PAC, Macdonald Papers, Volume 529, Macdonald to Bishop of Hamilton, March 25, 1890 (private).

4. R. A. Hill, "A Note on Newspaper Patronage in Canada During the Late 1850's and Early 1860's," *Canadian Historical Review*, XLIX, I (March, 1968), 44-59; see also P. B. Waite, *The Life and Times of Confederation* (Toronto: University of Toronto Press, 1962), pp. 8-11.

5. See page 14 for fuller discussion of this point.

6. J. M. S. Careless, *The Union of the Canadas* (Toronto: McClelland and Stewart, 1967), p. 200.

7. Joseph Dufresne was MPP for Montcalm. He was a Conservative.

8. Toronto *Globe*, June 5, 1856, reporting debates of June 3.

9 See A. W. Rasporich, "The Development of Political and Social Ideas in the Province of Canada, 1848-58," Ph.D. Thesis, University of Manitoba, 1970, p. 348. The relevant dates for *La Minerve* are November 11, 14, 18, 1857; January 23, March 28, April 3, 1858.

10. R. A. Hill, "The English-speaking minority of Lower Canada, the press, and federal union, 1856-1860: a study in public opinion," M.A. Thesis, McGill University, 1966, p. 85. See Montreal *Gazette*, April 28, 1856, for an English summary of Dorion's speech.

11. Quebec *Gazette*, July 12, 1858, reporting Galt's speech of July 5, in Hill, *op.cit.*, p. 116.

12. See, for example, *infra*, Section 1, Document Nos. 38, 39.

13. Hill, *op.cit.*, p. 120.

14. W. M. Whitelaw, *The Maritimes and Canada before Confederation* (Toronto: Oxford University Press, 1934), p. 128.

15. Colonial Office 217, Mulgrave to Lytton, December 30, 1858 (confidential).

16. Colonial Office 194, Bannerman to Lytton, February 24, 1859.

17. W. L. Morton, *The Critical Years* (Toronto: McClelland and Stewart, 1964), pp. 80-82.

Guide To Documents

In the documents that follow the Guide to Documents the author has occasionally used a short paraphrase to sum up sections of the original document. It thus seemed sensible to put all direct quotations inside quotation marks. Documents so quoted conform in spelling, grammar and punctuation to the originals. Since **Canadian History Through the Press** *is, in a limited sense, a history of Canadian journalism, it has seemed advisable to preserve contemporary usage, however questionable it might appear to be, in order to illustrate the changing quality of Canadian journalistic writing.*

Section I British North America

A. *The Atlantic Colonies, 1854-1863*

23. The Intercolonial Railroad. *Morning News*, Saint John, Friday, June 12, 1857.

24. The Cost of Federal Union. *Morning News*, Saint John, Wednesday, August 25, 1858.

25. The Intercolonial Railway. *Standard*, St. Andrews, Wednesday, October 1, 1862.

26. Railway Agreement broken. *Morning Chronicle*, Halifax, Thursday, October 8, 1863.

27. Hope of Union fading? *Acadian Recorder*, Halifax, Saturday, November 7, 1863.

B. *The Province of Canada, 1856-1863*

28. Opinions on Federal Union. *Gazette*, Montreal, Saturday, April 26, 1856.

29. Union of the Colonies from a national viewpoint. *La Patrie*, Montreal, Monday, November 3, 1856.

30. Federation or Closer Union of the Canadas? *Le Pays*, Montreal, Saturday, February 7, 1857.

31. Federal Union: the Politician's game? *Daily Colonist*, Toronto, Tuesday, September 22, 1857.

32. Concerning the North American Provinces and Federal Union.

33. Confederation of the Provinces. *La Patrie*, Montreal, Saturday, October 17, 1857.

34. Confederation: Canada at the crossroads. *Gazette*, Montreal, Saturday, April 17, 1858.

35. The Impracticable Double Majority. *Daily Colonist*, Toronto, May 22, 1858.

36. By what Policy are we to be governed? *Daily Colonist*, Toronto, Wednesday, June 30, 1858.

37. Speech by Galt on Confederation. *Daily Colonist*, Toronto, Tuesday, July 6, 1858.

38. Comment on Galt's Speech. *Leader*, Toronto, Tuesday, July 6, 1858.

39. Upper Canada and Federation: indecision of the Government. *Daily Colonist*, Toronto, Tuesday, July 6, 1858.

40. Freedom of the Press. *Daily Colonist*, Toronto, Monday, July 19, 1858.

41. Winds of Change needed. *Daily Colonist*, Toronto, Monday, August 2, 1858.

42. Galt's vision of a united Canada. *Pilot*, Montreal, Thursday, August 19, 1858.

43. Confederation and the People: fickleness of the public. *Daily Colonist*, Toronto, Tuesday, August 31, 1858.

44. A Federal Union: its nature, form and consequences. *British Colonist*, Toronto, Tuesday, October 26, 1858.

45. Lower Canada and Union: view of the minority. *Mercury*, Quebec, Saturday, May 28, 1859.

46. Lower Canada and Union: need for constitutional change. *Transcript*, Montreal, Thursday, July 14, 1859.

47. A union of the British American Colonies. *Stratford Beacon*, Stratford, Friday, August 21, 1857.

48. Confederation: what are its advantages? *Weekly Herald*, Montreal, Saturday, May 8, 1858.

49. Opposition to the Intercolonial Railroad. *Globe*, Toronto, Friday, October 8, 1858.

50. What would a Federation accomplish? *London Free Press,* London, Thursday, November 11, 1858.

51. Is a Federal Union required? *London Free Press,* London, Thursday, November 25, 1858.

52. The Mission a failure. *Perth Courier,* Perth, Friday, November 19, 1858.

53. The death of Confederation? *Weekly Herald,* Montreal, Saturday, February 12, 1859.

54. Federation: a means of dealing with Lower Canada. *Globe,* Toronto, Monday, July 11, 1859.

55. Quo vadis, O Canada? *Sarnia Observer,* Sarnia, Friday, October 21, 1859.

56. A blueprint for Federation. *Perth Courier,* Perth, Friday, November 4, 1859.

57. Speech by Sheppard. *Globe,* Toronto, Friday, November 11, 1859.

58. Federation: the need for clarity. *Globe,* Toronto, Saturday, November 12, 1859.

59. Brown and Federation. *Globe,* Toronto, Wednesday, November 16, 1859.

60. The choices facing the Colonies. *Transcript,* Montreal, Tuesday, November 15, 1859.

61. Lack of obstacles to Federation. *Globe,* Toronto, Friday, November 25, 1859.

62. The price of Provincialism. *Stratford Beacon,* Stratford, Friday, December 2, 1859.

63. French-Canadian pessimism over Confederation. *L'Ordre,* Montreal, Friday, May 4, 1860.

64. Inconsistency of the Government toward Federation. *Weekly Herald,* Saturday, May 26, 1860.

65. Federation: the great unknown. *Transcript,* Montreal, Saturday, November 10, 1860.

66. Support for the creation of the Northwest into a separate colony. *Leader,* Toronto, Friday, January 27, 1860.

67. A prescient forecast of the Coalition of 1864. *London Free Press,* London, Wednesday, June 6, 1860.

68. Growing pressure to deal with the question of Federation. *Gazette,* Montreal, Monday, November 19, 1860.

69. Lower Canada and Federation. *L'Ordre,* Montreal, Monday, March 11, and Friday, March 22, 1861.

70. French-Canadian support for the Intercolonial Railway. *La Minerve,* Montreal, Tuesday, September 16, 1862.

71. The need for a decisive policy. *Leader,* Toronto, Tuesday, October 14, 1862.

72. The Intercolonial Railway and Nationalism. *Leader,* Toronto, Saturday, October 25, 1862.

73. Questioning the advantages of the proposed Intercolonial Railway. *Weekly Dispatch,* St. Thomas, Thursday, November 13, 1862.

74. The Conservatives' attitude toward the Intercolonial Railway. *Morning Chronicle,* Quebec, Monday, January 19, 1863.

75. Criticism of the Government's shifting policy toward the Intercolonial Railway. *Leader,* Toronto, Friday, October 2, 1863.

76. A Lower Canada view of Nova Scotian attitudes. *Quebec Daily News,* Quebec, Saturday, November 17, 1863.

77. Sincerity of the Government toward the Intercolonial Railway project questioned. *Quebec Daily News,* Quebec, Saturday, December 5, 1863.

78. Federation: the destiny of Canada. *Globe*, Toronto, Wednesday, November 25, 1863.

C. *The Northwest, 1859-1863*

79. Position of Red River in Colonial Federation. *Nor'Wester*, Red River, Friday, February 1, 1861.

80. American proclivities in Red River. *Nor'Wester*, Red River, Wednesday, February 5, 1862.

81. Need to settle the claims of the Hudson's Bay Company. *Nor'Wester*, Red River, Wednesday, May 28, 1862.

Section II British North America, 1864-1867

A. *Colonists and Conferences, April-December, 1864*

1. Discontent with the present Union. *Aurora Banner*, Aurora, Friday, April 1, 1864.

2. Plea for stronger leadership. *Quebec Daily News*, Quebec, Thursday, June 16, 1864.

3. Brown and the charge of inconsistency. *Globe*, Toronto, Saturday, June 18, 1864.

4. On George Brown's high-mindedness. *Quebec Daily News*, Quebec, Monday, June 20, 1864.

5. The Reform party and Federal Union. *Globe*, Toronto, Wednesday, June 22, 1864.

6. Brown's Speech to Parliament. *Globe*, Toronto, Thursday, June 23, 1864.

7. The surprise and suddenness of Confederation, even in Canada, *Quebec Daily News*, Quebec, Friday, June 24, 1864.

8. Present need for men of principle in Government. *Hastings Chronicle*, Belleville, Wednesday, July 20, 1864.

9. Canada Letter, July 13, 1864. *Weekly British Colonist*, Victoria, Tuesday, August 23, 1864.

10. On the Maritime Union debate in the Legislature. *Halifax Citizen*, Halifax, Tuesday, March 29, 1864.

11. Prince Edward Island and Union. *Islander*, Charlottetown, Friday, June 24, 1864.

12. Federation: a panacea or an ideal? *Daily Evening Globe*, Saint John, Monday, June 30, 1864.

13. A Review of the situation with regard to Federation. *Head Quarters*, Fredericton, Wednesday, July 6, 1864.

14. Support for the union of British America. *Acadian Recorder*, Halifax, Saturday, July 30, 1864.

15. Caution urged concerning the question of union. *Daily Evening Globe*, Saint John, Thursday, August 4, 1864.

16. Political expediency rejected in Federation. *Morning Chronicle*, Halifax, Thursday, August 4, 1864.

17. The larger issues involved in Union. *Quebec Daily News*, Quebec, Tuesday, August 16, 1864.

18. A New Brunswick view of internal Canadian politics. *Morning Telegraph*, Saint John, Saturday, August 13, 1864.

B. Colonial reactions to the Quebec Resolutions

44. Federation differs from the United States system. *Globe,* Toronto, Monday, August 1, 1864.

45. Federation: a system best suited to Canadian diversity. *Vindicator,* Oshawa, Wednesday, August 31, 1864.

46. Reservations with regard to Federation. *Spectator,* Hamilton, Monday, October 31, 1864.

47. War clouds and Confederation. *Morning Telegraph,* Saint John, Friday, December 30, 1864.

48. Vitality of the Federation issue in the Maritimes. *Intelligencer,* Belleville, Friday, January 20, 1865.

49. British American attitudes to Government and Society. *Evening Journal,* St. Catherines, Wednesday, February 22, 1865.

50. Two views of the Quebec debates. *Leader,* Toronto, Wednesday, January 25, and Tuesday, February 28, 1865.

51. A further view of the Confederation debate at Quebec. *Stratford Beacon,* Stratford, Friday, March 3, 1865.

52. Which course should Canada adopt? *Prescott Telegraph,* Prescott, Wednesday, March 8, 1865.

53. Setback for Union. *Globe,* Toronto, Friday, March 24, 1865.

54. Canadian vulnerability in the face of possible United States aggression. *Evening Times,* Hamilton, in the *London Evening Advertiser,* Wednesday, March 15, 1865.

55. Fear of severance of links with Britain. *Northern Advance,* Barrie, Wednesday, July 5, 1865.

56. A changed situation. *Stratford Beacon,* Stratford, Friday, September 28, 1866.

57. Macdonald and Federal Union. *Citizen,* Ottawa, Friday, September 29, 1865.

58. Confederation: the only answer. *Le Canadien,* Quebec, Monday, August 1, 1864.

59. Legislative Union rather than Federal Union. *Gazette,* Montreal, Wednesday, August 24, 1864.

60. Federalism: a protection of French-Canadian interests. *La Minerve,* Montreal, Tuesday, August 30, 1864.

61. Support for a Legislative Union. *Gazette,* Montreal, Friday, September 2, 1864.

62. What Federation must not be. *True Witness and Catholic Chronicle,* Montreal, Friday, September 23, 1864.

63. Provincial Rights and Federalism. *Le Courrier du Canada,* Quebec, Monday, October 10, 1864.

64. Federalism: another name for Legislative Union? *Le Pays,* Montreal, Tuesday, November 8, 1864.

65. Confederation X. *Le Courrier du Canada,* Quebec, Monday, December 26, 1864.

66. A European view of Federalism. *L'Ordre,* Montreal, Monday, January 2, 1865.

67. A French-Canadian view of the necessity of change. *La Minerve,* Montreal, Saturday, February 18, 1865.

68. Change has to come. *Gazette,* Montreal, Friday, March 3, 1865.

69. Confederation and American Confederation. *L'Ordre,* Montreal, Wednesday, June 7, and Friday, June 9, 1865.

70. Lower Canada's fear of outside decisions. *Le Canadien,* Quebec, Friday, May 18, 1866.

71. A change of view. *L'Ordre*, Montreal, Wednesday, June 6, 1866.

72. No support for Union. *Patriot*, St. John's, Tuesday, November 29, 1864.

73. The Confederate broom will clean up political life. *Day Book*, St. John's, Wednesday, November 30, 1864.

74. Newfoundland's fears of the burdens of Confederation. *Patriot*, St. John's, Tuesday, December 6, 1864.

75. The loss of Independence: a disadvantage? *Newfoundlander*, St. John's, Thursday, January 12, 1865.

76. Mercantile attitudes to Confederation. *Patriot*, St. John's, Saturday, August 12, 1865.

77. The Newfoundland election of 1865 and the question of Union. *Patriot*, St. John's, Saturday, September 2, 1865.

78. Local interests and Federation: a different view. *Courier*, St. John's, Saturday, July 14, 1866.

79. The Newfoundland press and Union. *Morning Chronicle*, St. John's, Saturday, December 22, 1866.

80. A pro-Confederate view. *Public Ledger*, St. John's, Friday, November 30, 1866.

81. Attitude of Prince Edward Island to Federation. *Examiner*, Charlottetown, Monday, January 30, 1865.

82. Suspicion of Tupper's motives. *Halifax Citizen*, Halifax, Saturday, November 5, 1864.

83. The issues involved as seen by a Nova Scotian newspaper. *Yarmouth Herald*, Yarmouth, Thursday, November 17, 1864.

84. Federation and the question of the frontier. *Morning Chronicle*, Halifax, Saturday, November 19, 1864.

85. Dissatisfaction over the limitations of the Confederation scheme. *Halifax Citizen*, Halifax, Saturday, November 19, 1864.

86. Opponents of Confederation. *Evening Reporter*, Halifax, Saturday, December 10, 1864.

87. The financial aspect of Union. *Bullfrog*, Halifax, Saturday, December 17, 1864.

88. A plea for the end of localism. *Unionist and Halifax Journal*, Halifax, Monday, January 23, 1865.

89. Confederation: fear of what it could involve. *Morning Chronicle*, Halifax, Monday, January 30, 1865.

90. Provincialism: the path to success. *Morning Chronicle*, Halifax, Wednesday, February 8, 1865.

91. Immediate Union. *British Colonist*, Halifax, Thursday, February 28, 1865.

92. The future of Nova Scotia under Confederation. *Morning Chronicle*, Halifax, Tuesday, December 12, 1865.

93. Howe's Speech at Windsor, Nova Scotia. *Morning Chronicle*, Halifax, Saturday, May 19, 1866.

94. Thoughts on Confederation. *Yarmouth Tribune*, Yarmouth, Wednesday, June 27, 1866.

95. Confederation and Local Legislatures: the continuation of a bad system. *Daily Evening Globe*, Saint John, Monday, October 17, 1864.

96. Will Confederation make the local legislatures redundant? *Morning Freeman*, Saint John, Thursday, November 3, 1864.

Section I

British North America, 1854-1863

A. The Atlantic Colonies, 1854-1863

The first debate of any substance on Union of the Colonies took place in the Nova Scotia Legislative Assembly in February, 1854. J. W. Johnston, leader of the Conservative opposition, proposed resolutions asking for "the union or confederation of the British North American Provinces, on just principles," and which "while calculated to perpetuate their connexion with the parent state, will promote their advancement and prosperity, increase their strength and influence, and elevate their position." Johnston had talked to Lord Durham at Quebec in 1838, and had favoured, as Durham had, a general colonial union at that time. In 1854 Johnston still preferred a legislative union rather than a federal one.

Johnston's resolutions never passed the House. They were not defeated, but consideration of them was postponed. This postponement was owing partly to Howe's preference for a federation of the British Empire, and partly from the pressure of other business. In any case the resolutions were not taken up again in 1855. The outbreak of the Crimean War and issues surrounding the new reciprocity treaty with the United States inhibited further debate on Union of the Colonies.

In the years that followed there appeared a growing sense of the necessity for drawing the Colonies together. There was some disillusionment in Nova Scotia over how responsible government worked in colonies with a small population, riddled with political and religious quarrels. But there were other issues as well; the threat, in 1857, to give France further privileges on Newfoundland's French Shore, the question of the future of the Hudson's Bay Territory in the West, and, after 1860, a growing number of issues with the United States brought on by the Civil War.

In all of this the Nova Scotia newspapers take what can fairly be described as the lead in the Atlantic colonies. But none of these newspapers ever got down to the details of how such a union, whether legislative or federal, might be constructed on an equitable basis. It is true that not a few Maritimers, especially the Nova Scotians, thought of Union of the Colonies as a legislative union, pure and simple. But even those who did urge federal union seemed quite in the dark about how, specifically, it might be put together. In the end, that task was taken on by the Canadians, and their solutions reflected, inevitably, issues and difficulties in the Province of Canada.

The Growing Sense of the Necessity of Union

1 WILKINS AND UNION

British Colonist, Halifax
Tuesday, June 13, 1854

Here is M. I. Wilkins' speech on J. W. Johnston's resolutions for a union of the colonies. The debate began in the Assembly on February 23, 1854. Wilkins' speech was given on Saturday, February 25, 1854. His argument in favour of union, and against the federal principle, was to persist in Nova Scotia.

"A union of the B.N.A. [*sic*] Colonies I believe to be indispensable. . . . We may become independent without casting off our allegiance. Colonies are like children . . . when they arrive at maturity they require different treatment. . . . They have a right to look about the world and set up for themselves. . . . But does it follow from this that all connection between them and their parents must cease? —By no means. . . . With regard to a federal union I will waste few words. There is an old saying but a very true one that 'Union is strength'. That the North America Colonies ought to be united there can be no rational doubt, but the union should be perfect, unqualified and absolute. They should be so incorporated that their interests should be identical. The Canadian, the New Brunswicker, the Nova Scotian and the inhabitants of the other Canadas should be so united as to feel, to know, and to be assured, that they are for ever henceforth to be one and the same people. A federal union would produce the very opposite effect. . .It is not the first time that the neighboring confederation has felt the inconvenience of this paradoxical kind of discordant union, and in all probability the principal sources of final revolution and disruption in the United States. . . . I feel convinced that representa-tion in the Imperial Parliament cannot be successfully resorted to. . . . "

2 UNION OF THE COLONIES

Acadian Recorder, Halifax
Saturday, March 4, 1854

"We have had three very flowery speeches, in the House, on this subject, and, for all practical purposes, it remains where it was at first. We hope the question has not got its *quietus* for the session. Not that we are particularly desirous of hearing three more speeches upon it, each occupying a whole day; but it is extremely desirous that the House should take some active step towards the accomplishment of this great, national object. It is to be feared that the majority of members will not feel disposed to deal with this question with that serious attention which its importance demands. It is something quite beyond the petty arena on which they have been accustomed to perform. . . . It cannot, with any kind of consistency, be made a *party* question; consequently many House members cannot see that it is a question for them to deliberate upon at all.

"It is nevertheless very extraordinary that the subject of Union of the Colonies has never been brought before a Provincial Legislature. . . . Probably there is not, at this day, a public man of respectable standing, in British America, who is opposed to that Union. Then why not have it at once? The initiative must be taken somewhere. There is no reason then why Nova Scotia should not take the lead. . . .

"It is useless to think of recounting, in one short article, a tenth of the arguments which might be urged in favor of this measure. The wrangling and faction squabbling which take place daily, in our House of Assembly, are alone an unanswerable argument in its favour . . . Cannot those legislators unchain their minds *a little,* and let that *partizan* spirit grow into a *national* spirit? If we must have our-party Cabinets, our Wigs [sic] and Tories, and all the grand paraphernalia of imperial statesmanship, let us have some choice of the material to make them of, and a field upon which to manoeuvre them."

3 BRITISH AMERICAN NATIONALITY

Acadian Recorder, Halifax
Saturday, May 23, 1857

"Gradually and surely, and yet not slowly, the idea of British American Nationality is extending. . . . It is but little more than three years since the Honourable J. W. Johnston brought before our House of Assembly the question of a Union of these Provinces. That was the first effort of a British American statesman, in his public capacity, to deal practically with the subject. Already the idea of such a Union was familiar to the leading minds of the country and some of them had publicly advocated the measure as a means of our political regeneration; but the realization of their hopes was still regarded as something pending in the remote future. The movement made in the Nova Scotia House of Assembly, in 1854, showed that there were men who believed the time to have arrived when practical measures should be taken. The influence of their example shows that it only required the initiative to be thus taken in order to waken up all British America to a belief that the time for action in the matter was rapidly approaching, if it had not already arrived. Since then, the subject has been discussed by most of the leading presses of the Provinces. . . . "

4 UNION OF THE PROVINCES

Morning Sun, Halifax
Friday, February 3, 1858

This article was probably written by Joseph Howe.

" . . . this question of the Union of the Provinces is one of great magnitude and importance. It is the question of questions. . . . Responsible Government has done much for all the Provinces, but there is much more to be done. We shall be mere Colonists till that much has been achieved. Every day we hear of some Nova Scotian or New Brunswicker winning distinction abroad, while every day we see Mr. Johnston* himself, with his gray locks floating in the air, working for his bread amid the stifling atmosphere of a Colonial Court House, with no prize before him but a seat on the bench, while some Lord's son, or Member of Parliament's brother, without a tithe of his talent, or a twentieth part of his Colonial experience, is sent to reign over him [i.e., as Lieutenant-Governor], in his own country."

*J. W. Johnston was Premier of Nova Scotia from 1838 to 1847 and from 1857 to 1860. He was appointed judge in 1863.

5 THE PRESS AND UNION

Acadian Recorder, Halifax
Saturday, March 27, 1858

"For years, we were, in this particular, almost alone among the members of the British American press. Many indeed of our contemporaries re-echoed the sentiments expressed by us, but without pursuing the subject further on their own account; others remained totally silent on the subject. . . . Everything tended to show that the press generally, like the leading statesmen of all parties in the Provinces, was favorably disposed towards the measure; but it did not evince a sense of the pressing necessity for immediate action being taken in the matter. The Union was looked upon only as an approaching necessity yet distant, the consideration of which could be postponed, for the present, in favor of other matters which were really of a local, or comparatively insignificant nature.

"We are happy to be able to say that this season of lukewarmness appears now to be past, or very nearly so."

6 DISILLUSIONMENT WITH RESPONSIBLE GOVERNMENT

Morning Journal, Halifax
Friday, December 23, 1859

"So far as one may judge they [the colonial legislatures of British North America] all expect an exceedingly stormy session. The whole of them are adrift upon what was at one time thought to be thoroughly understood in these British North American Provinces, viz.:—Responsible Government. But we think it must be clear to the commonest comprehension, that the Colonists either do not understand the new system, or that it is not suited to the peculiar circumstances in which we are placed. It cannot be denied that the partizan spirit which for the last twenty years, and upwards, rent these Provinces asunder, thereby hindering their advancement in material progress, has given place to religious animosities of even a more inveterate character. Heaven only knows where this state of things is to end."

7 POLITICAL LIFE IN NOVA SCOTIA

Evening Reporter, Halifax
Tuesday, August 21, 1860

This editorial is copied from the Toronto *Leader,* whose editor had been visiting the Maritime provinces.

"This practice [in Nova Scotia] of changing subordinate officers [*i.e.,* in the civil service] with the change of government makes politics a struggle for existence. Men engaged in them are fighting not merely for position, but for bread. The intensity of such a life-and-death struggle is evidenced by the bitterness of political contests. We think ourselves bad in Canada; but we are left in the rear by Nova Scotia. Roebuck once said he had been condemned, for his sins, to live in a colony; and there is little doubt that the smaller the colony the greater the punishment. Public men are not unaware of the degradation of their politics; and many feel the necessity for some change that shall give them increased dignity and importance. . . .

"Some are inclined to favor a Union of the Maritime Provinces only, as being the most natural or as a stepping stone to an ultimate Union of all the Provinces. There are persons both here [Nova Scotia] and in New Brunswick who take this view of the matter; but some of them would accept a Federal Union at once, if it could be brought about. . . . It is very generally felt that these North American Provinces, which, united would occupy the position of the third commercial power in the world are deprived of their legitimate position and influence by their isolation; that their politics are dwarfed by the contracted sphere in which the public men are obliged to move, and that the field of honorable ambition is unduly contracted."

8 THE REWARD OF POLITICAL MERIT IN THE PROVINCES

Evening Reporter, Halifax
Tuesday, September 17, 1861

"The rewards for political merit are so few as to afford little encouragement for a man of talent and ambition to throw his whole energies into the political arena. After years of unremitting labor and exposure to all those annoyances that must be encountered in a state of heated politics like ours, he may attain a seat in the Cabinet, or, perhaps the leadership of a party. . . . a man in entering the conflict of politics must make up his mind deliberately to spend the best days of his manhood on a hotly-contested field; and, as likely as not, find himself in the end with hopes blasted and impoverished; all that is left him being, perhaps, the reputation of some fair share of statesmanlike sagacity and ability — but a poor source of income in this practical, money-making age . . . .

"The results of such a state of politics are obvious. It has a tendency to drive into private life the best men in the community, and place in power those who care nothing for the public advantage except when their own ambition and emolument are engaged. . . . We must have the political arena of these Provinces enlarged. . . . By having a Union of the Provinces, simply — we care not whether it be a Union of the Maritime Colonies or of all the Provinces. . . . we may hope to see larger and nobler motives prompting our statesmen. . . . "

9 OUR FUTURE: WHAT SHALL IT BE?

Colonial Empire, Saint John
Wednesday, October 1, 1862

"The Colonial Empire of Great Britain is rapidly approaching a most important crisis in its history. . . . They are fast merging toward the confines of political manhood. They have already reached a position which renders it a pressing necessity to initiate important changes in their external relations and their political form. Neither the proper development of their varied resources nor the just gratification of the laudable aspirations of their people is compatible with the lengthened continuance of their present relations to each other and to the mother country. Their commune with each other hampered by discordant tariffs, and by a variant currency; their manufacturing interests few and feebly prosecuted; without constitutional means of acting effectively in concert for the general good; isolated, feeble, insignificant in their separation; the time has come for them to seek or assume a status commensurate with their real importance, and accordant with the requirements of their glowing future. . . . This great country stretches away from the shores of the Atlantic to the waters of the wide Pacific."

The Importance of Union in the Light of Relations with Great Britain and the United States

10 COLONIAL SUPPORT FOR NEWFOUNDLAND

Newfoundlander, St. John's
Thursday, April 2, 1857

The support given by the mainland colonies to Newfoundland, in March, 1857, in its quarrel with the British government over the draft Anglo-French Convention on the French Shore, marked a first step in Newfoundland's look to the west.

"The Newfoundland delegates are now in Halifax, where their reception has been most cordial, and strongest sympathy evinced in the object of their mission. . . . Our own unanimous, manful, and indignant rejection of the proposal, and the strenuous support of our Sister Colonies, will force upon the British Government a stern practical lesson. . . .

"This Delegation is looked on as the first step towards some movement in favor of some means by which the Provinces may act together on all subjects affecting their interests."

11 CLOSER TIES BETWEEN THE MARITIME COLONIES

Newfoundlander, St. John's
Thursday, April 16, 1857

In mid-April, 1857 came the announcement that the British Government had dropped the proposed Convention with France. Not only had Nova Scotia and New Brunswick supported Newfoundland, but Prince Edward Island and Canada also.

"We cannot soon forget our obligations to our Sister Colonies of Nova Scotia and New Brunswick, who have identified themselves with our struggle. Whether their aid was or was not needful to the result is not the question now — we have but to remember that they gave it with earnestness and with generous measure, when it appeared to be of moment, and our gratitude must be proportional to their cordial desires in our regard."

12 THE HUDSON'S BAY COMPANY

Morning News, Saint John
Friday, April 23, 1858

"In the lower Provinces there is too much apathy with regard to this matter [of the Hudson's Bay Company in the West.] Canada is nobly struggling to break up the hateful monopoly that keeps so much territory and so many people in bondage, while we are looking on [as] uninterested spectators, seemingly careless of whether she succeeds or not, as though the final issue were of no importance to our future welfare. That this is decidely wrong needs no argument of ours to prove.

". . . . It may not to-day nor to-morrow be of interest to us what becomes of the Hudson's Bay Territory; but in a very few years when our political condition will have assumed a new form, when we will find ourselves depending more on our own resources than we do at present, and competing with a powerful neighbor for the commerce of the globe, it will be apparent then that every inch of ground we possess will be wanted."

13 QUESTIONING THE CONNECTION

Morning News, Saint John
Wednesday, June 2, 1858

"While, indeed, a feeling of respect, of love, and of admiration for the

Mother Country, may ever be retained in Canada, we question whether there is loyalty of sufficient depth to prevent her dissolving her connection with Britain to-morrow, if it could be proved that such dissolution would in any way enrich or benefit her. And, further, we question whether this Federal Union which is so much talked of as to almost appear a reality, is not to be the beginning of the end of British rule in North America. . . .

"The experience of history tells us that Colonies cannot be Colonies forever; and Canada in time will assume that character among the Nations of the world which her position, her wealth, and her intelligence will entitle her to. . . . Of course that time is not yet — nor will it likely be in our day and generation."

14 BRITISH – AMERICAN INTERESTS IN JEOPARDY

Acadian Recorder, Halifax
Saturday, September 24, 1859

British American interests are in jeopardy, said the Halifax *Acadian Recorder.* In 1857 there was the French Shore crisis in Newfoundland, and now there is the American claim to San Juan Island on the west coast. Great Britain has done this sort of thing before; we have lost the northern half of Maine, the southern quarter of British Columbia, and the inshore fisheries of Nova Scotia to the United States.

"Why is this? Mainly because we British North Americans are not true to ourselves; because, possessing the elements of a great nation, we choose to remain split up in sections, estranged from each other objectless. [*sic*] powerless. Were these Colonies from Newfoundland to Vancouver inclusive, united under a single Government, whether Federal, or one involving a firmer consolidation, no 'intrepid' Harney would venture to make such aggression upon our soil as that which has lately been made on the Pacific Coast. Until we have decided upon such a Union, we must expect to be treated without the tenderness vouchsafed to a Colony and without the respect accorded to an independent power. . . . "

15 UNION OF THE COLONIES

British Colonist, Halifax
Tuesday, September 4, 1860

"This *unity*, is the very fact which was sought for and obtained by Newfoundland in 1857 to strengthen her hands against the attempted *convention*. What did she do? She sent a deputation to Canada and the other Provinces for a *combined expression* of feeling and *united* resistance to a wrong! She succeeded, and the Convention fell to the ground. A striking lesson for the future, to unite and be strong. May all profit by it, and let the watchword for all be Provincial Union."

16 THE AMERICAN CRISIS

Acadian Recorder, Halifax
Saturday, December 22, 1860

Lessons from the American crisis for British North American constitution makers: a perceptive editorial.

"Whether the Union of the States is dissolved this year, or not, we British Americans may draw a salutary lesson from the troubles now existing there. If the dissolution takes place, it will be owing . . . to the absurd Federal Constitution of that country — to the fact that the Union consists in a Federation of *Sovereign* States. We British Americans hope to effect a Union of these Colonies. When we talk of a *Federation* of them, we should be certain of our own meaning. As we have repeatedly endeavored to show, a Federation upon the Yankee model cannot but prove a failure. A house divided against itself *will* fall, prop it as we may. In our Federation, if we ever have one, the parts must be all entirely subordinated to the whole. The power of the separate Provinces must be limited and special; those of the general Government, unlimited and general."

17 THE OPINION OF CHARLES TUPPER

Evening Reporter, Halifax
Thursday, January 23, 1862

Report of a lecture given January 22, 1862 at Temperance Hall by Charles Tupper.

"It must be evident to every one that as we are now situated we are entirely without name or nationality, destitute of all influence and of the means of occupying that position to which we may justly aspire. What is a British American but a man dependent on an Empire which, however glorious, gives him no share or interest in it! The past is pregnant with illustrations of the truth of this assertion. What voice had New Brunswick, when a large portion of her country was sliced off and given to the States by the British Government, without any reference to her whatever? [Webster-Ashburton Treaty, 1842] . . .

"We can have no dependence on the everchanging dicta of Downing Street."

18 SPEECH BY JOSEPH HOWE

Morning Chronicle, Halifax
Tuesday, September 30, 1862

Howe in a speech at Niagara, Canada West, September 18, 1862, supported the right of the Canadians to defeat any and all Militia Bills if they so chose, and without recriminations from the British. The speech was reported in the Toronto *Globe*, and is here reproduced from the Halifax paper that supported Howe and Howe's government.

Howe said he had had a letter from Tilley in New Brunswick recently.

"How are you in Nova Scotia? Are you prepared for independence? Have you read Goldwin Smith's letters [in the London *Daily News*]?' He (Mr. Howe) wrote back — 'No! I have not read Goldwin Smith's letters. I am prepared for anything. Nova Scotia will float, if the devil himself cuts the townline.' (Great cheering and laughter.) . . .

"We did not desire premature independence . . . but, if our connection with England, Scotland, and Ireland was to be preserved, it must be an honorable connection, one we can maintain without exposing ourselves to reproach for exercising the powers which our constitution gives us. (Cheers.) He would remind those men who had used offensive language towards these Provinces, that people would sometimes submit to a great deal of injustice who would not bear a taunt or an insult. . . . If they were as familiar with these Canadian forests as he was, they would know that a single nipping frost could convert all the beautiful verdure we see to-day into vermil tints of a very different complexion. (Cheers.)"

Howe looked forward to the Intercolonial railway, and to the time when "this great Province of Canada would be connected with the Provinces below, and when a man would feel that to be a British American was to be a citizen of a country which included all these fertile lands, all these inexhaustible fisheries, all this immense marine, carrying to all seas the flag of Old England, if she would let us, and if she will not let us, the flag of British America, bearing to foreign countries the lineaments, the enterprise and the spirit of Britons, and the civilization of British America, of which, he trusted, none of us need be much ashamed. (Loud cheers.)"

Attitudes to the Province of Canada and to Canadian Issues

19 OTTAWA, THE NEW CAPITAL

Acadian Recorder, Halifax
Saturday, February 13, 1858

Leading editorial on the new capital of Canada.

"The Royal *fiat* has gone forth, declaring the city of Ottawa the future capital of British North America . . . . it appeared obvious that the seat of Government should be chosen with a view to the place selected being the capital, not merely of Canada, but of the whole United Provinces. In this view of the case, we, in the Lower Provinces, were quite as much interested in the result of Her Majesty's choice as the Canadians themselves. . . . If, as to the seat of Government in this Province, a dispute were to arise between Halifax, Windsor, Truro, and Pictou, and the dispute were terminated by Upper Musquodoboit being pitched upon as the future capital, the selection would be just about as judicious as this. . . . We hope Ottawa will not be the permanent capital of British America."

---

20 OPINIONS ON FEDERAL UNION

Morning Chronicle, Halifax
Thursday, December 6, 1860

"The 'extravagance', and worse than extravagance of public men in Canada, is not a mere chimera but a fatal reality . . . and we in this Province think it prudent to hesitate. . . .

"A Union — not a Federal, but a Legislative Union — of the maritime Provinces, is quite a different matter." It is feasible. "But a union with Canada we do not regard as possible, at present. We no longer occupy the same ground, respectively, as we did in 1851. Then the different Provinces were so nearly on a footing of equality, as regards their commercial and financial affairs, that an equitable adjustment of their several interests would have been a matter of no great difficulty. Then, the offer of Earl Grey, of imperial assistance for the imperial road, — an offer, by the way, which has never been withdrawn, — held out a powerful inducement to united railway action, which might have led to a federal union. Now, all this is changed; and changed in such a way, and by such agencies, as to lead people in the Lower Provinces to regard with but small measure of esteem or respect, the Government men of Canada."

35

21 A MARITIME RESPONSE TO MACDONALD'S SPEECH ON CONFEDERATION

Evening Reporter, Halifax
Tuesday, May 14, 1861

The American Civil War had broken out on April 12, 1861. A week later, John A. Macdonald took up the theme of British North American Confederation in the Canadian legislature.

"When the present Government of Canada enunciated their policy in 1858, they were understood to be the advocates of a union of the British American Provinces. Mr. Galt, the Inspector-General, has, indeed, been always considered one of the leading exponents of that great question. The administration, however, have never taken any action in the matter, or, indeed expressed any particular opinion for these several years past, to the regret of the many persons who see in a union the true remedy for the many political evils that are agitating Canada and many of the other Provinces. Latterly, however, the Canadian Press has been constantly dwelling on the necessity of some initiatory action. . . . [Here follows part of Macdonald's speech.] It is to be hoped that this expression of opinion of Mr. Macdonald is but the precursor of some energetic action . . . on the part of the Canadian Government."

22 CHANGING SENTIMENT WITH REGARD TO UNION

Morning Journal, Halifax
Wednesday, September 25, 1861

"Shortly after the visit of His Royal Highness, the Prince of Wales, to this continent [late summer and autumn of 1860], the proposed Union of the British North American Colonies created a great deal of discussion, in England, as well as in the Provinces. The Colonial Secretary [the Duke of Newcastle] was said to be favorably impressed with the idea. The leading English journals viewed it in a most auspicious light. And even the American newspapers, animated by the most friendly and disinterested motives, and almost nauseating in their professions of regard for our Queen, and the United Kingdom [especially after the visit of the Prince of Wales to the United States], had naught to say against it. . . . In more respects than one there has been a change in public sentiment since then. Our American contemporaries have abandoned their honeyed words. . . .

"The feeling in the Lower Provinces against a Union with Canada has rather increased than diminished. Even the prospects for an Inter-Colonial Railway . . . fail to awaken the desire for ties of a closer and more intimate nature. The unseemly political broils, and the past political history of Canada, with her rebellions, and riots, her Grand Trunk Railway, with its corrupting influence upon politicions [*sic*]; the national debt, which seems to increase as the snow-ball . . . are not pleasant matters for persons of a timid and unventuresome disposition to contemplate. At all events they fail to attract many into playing the lover. . . . "

The Intercolonial Railway and Union

23 THE INTERCOLONIAL RAILROAD

Morning News, Saint John
Friday, June 12, 1857

"We now come to speak of the probability and practicability of accomplishing that which everybody has at heart, who wishes for a union, consolidation and nationality of these Provinces — viz. an Inter-Colonial Railroad. . . . We are in a position then, to make an effort, for the consummation of this object. It only requires a movement on the part of one of the Colonial Governments, and we are quite satisfied that the others will join issue. Suppose we commence the *talk* in our Province. Here we have a new, strong, energetic, set of men at the head of affairs. In fact we have a Government powerful and influential enough to raise this Province from the dust, and contribute largely towards the union of British North America, in heart, sentiment and understanding."

24 THE COST OF FEDERAL UNION

Morning News, Saint John
Wednesday, August 25, 1858

"Preliminary to a British North American union we regard the building of the inter-Colonial Railroad to be an absolute condition — for there can be no union of feeling and sentiment, or harmony of understanding and action, while such physical difficulties as are geographically described, stand in the way of the people of Canada West and those of Nova Scotia, separated by a distance of 800 miles, and who can only communicate with one another through American territory. But aside from this there is much to be understood, much information to be obtained, by the people of these lower Provinces, ere they can adopt this hobby 'union' and consider it a boon favourable to their political and social interests. . . . will a Federal Union involve a Federal Debt, a Federal Tariff, and a Federal management of Public Works . . . ? . . . a Tariff that is applicable to Canada with a debt of six or eight millions [of pounds], would be exceedingly burdensome to New Brunswick with scarcely any debt at all. . . . Until informed, however, of the real facts of the case, and our mistake, if any pointed out, we shall imagine that this Federal Union business, however advantageous to Canada, will prove to be a rather costly luxury to the inhabitants of the lower regions who, many of them, imagine that as progress is the order of the day, every political change advocated is one calculated to promote the general good. . . . It would be as well, therefore, for the people of the Lower Provinces to think well before deciding upon a matter of such grave importance. Our leading statesmen in the Lower Provinces are anxious for this Federation. But the question is has not their ambition something to do with the desire? Their present arena (a small Colonial House of Assembly) is too circumscribed for a full display of their abilities. Their light, they consider, is hid under a bushel. . . . Many of our cotemporaries [*sic*] write upon this subject in approving terms; but they are all remarkably, perhaps sensibly, silent, when speculating upon the advantages, in giving us their opinion as to the cost the charge is likely to produce upon the Lower Provinces. . . . "

25 THE INTERCOLONIAL RAILWAY

Standard, St. Andrews
Wednesday, October 1, 1862

"The Intercolonial Railway is now the most important topic of the day as regards the future destiny of the North American Colonies; and now that there is a more vivid prospect of their connexion by means of such a railway which will strengthen and enhance their commercial interests, it may not be thought too visionary, to hope that the construction of the Railroad will be followed by a political confederation, such a union of the whole might be regarded as the one grand climax that has been steadily approaching us for years past, and which may be consummated by the present generation of politicians under the guidance of the Chief at Downing-Street."

26 RAILWAY AGREEMENT BROKEN

Morning Chronicle, Halifax
Thursday, October 8, 1863

Resentment in Nova Scotia, as in New Brunswick is manifest over what Maritimers certainly felt was the perfidy of the Sandfield Macdonald government of Canada in breaking the agreement on building the Intercolonial railway.

"If Canada, as is most evident, now repudiates her five-twelfths of the expense of constructing an Intercolonial Railway, what earthly use is there in further trifling, and in wasting our funds in any survey? . . . It is all up, and the sooner we of the lower Provinces begin to think and act for ourselves, independent of Canada, the better."

27 HOPE OF UNION FADING?

Acadian Recorder, Halifax
Saturday, November 7, 1863

The dissillusionment of one newspaper, long a supporter of Confederation, after the Intercolonial debacle of the autumn of 1863, is here ruefully expressed.

"There seems to be some stir in our press about that threadbare subject, Union of the Colonies . . . Are there any signs of political union among these British Colonies? Is not each Colony too busily occupied, are not the intellects of our statesmen too much pressed down by the grave cares of petty party bickerings [?] There is talk enough of union. Union of the Colonies is a popular fiddle to play on, and there are fools enough to dance. But what work is there for union. What Colonial man with a head on his shoulders, has done something — sacrificed something for such object? . . . The late Intercolonial action on the Railway question is a valuable lesson on this subject. . . .

"As Colonies we seem to be going in different political directions. We seem to be severing what ties there are between us. Perhaps there never was so much jealousy and bad feeling between these Colonies as at the present time. . . . This story [Union] we say is a capital one for stump speeches and newspaper flip-flap. We do not say that a political union would not be of service; but what we do say is that there seems less hope for any such project than ever there was. . . . "

B. The Province of Canada, 1856-1863

The driving force for change came from Canada West. The Reform party especially, led by George Brown, was by 1856 largely convinced that the existing constitution of the province could not, would not, work unless changes were made. These changes can be broadly comprehended under "rep. by pop." It is a nice question whether "rep. by pop." would have been satisfactory even had it been introduced; but as it was, the Reform party found in French-Canadian resistance to "rep. by pop." all the reasons that led Brown and others to insist even more vehemently upon having it.

The response of the Conservative party to this kind of pressure was to temporize, and one principal form of temporizing used was British North American union. It was harmless; it bespoke a sense of national grandeur, which was good; and it was believed impossible to realize within a generation, which was even better. It could be talked about without affecting the fortunes of a Conservative government, except possibly to improve them. Galt's proposals of July, 1858, made before he came into the government, were thus given rather short shrift, both by the Conservative government, and by the Assembly as a whole. After the double shuffle, however, after George Brown's fleeting summer government was refused a dissolution; after the awful iniquity of the double shuffle; after the cries of outrage that burst forth against Macdonald, the Conservatives, the Governor-General from a defeated and frustrated Reform party, Confederation of British North America was excellent politics for the Conservative party. Thus, in the fall of 1858, the Conservative government plunged cheerfully ahead with it, almost certainly aware it had little chance of being implemented, and knowing fully what a fine smoke-screen it made.

Federation of the Province of Canada, which the Reform party brought forward the following year, in 1859, was more sincerely felt and meant. It too was the result of political difficulties, but it was more realistic. It required only the approval of the legislature of the province and the concurrence of the Colonial Office and the British Parliament. It was thought to be cheap and easy. There were elements in the Reform party who felt it was conceived too narrowly, that there was no point in a federation of the Canadas without the

39

ambience of a larger nationality to go with it. For such Reform critics, of whom George Sheppard was the most trenchant, the only sensible course for the moment was the dissolution of the Union.

Brown was able to resist this, and persuade his party to do so at the Reform Convention of November, 1859, in Toronto. This saw the adoption of strong resolutions urging federation of the Province of Canada.

Thus, there had emerged, by the beginning of 1860, two sharply contrasted policies, British North American Confederation, the smokescreen policy of the Conservative party, and federation of Canada, the real policy of the Reform party. The type of federation conceived by each is, in general outline, perceptible. Galt's Confederation of 1858 was not unlike that of 1864, except in being rather less centralized. Brown's federation was thoroughly decentralized, giving, in fact, to the central government of a federated Province of Canada only a few essential general matters, like railways, canals, trade, post office.

Given these party positions, Canada West's attitudes to the Intercolonial Railway fall neatly into place. The Conservatives were not averse to the Intercolonial. They conceived it rather like an extension of the Grand Trunk. But they were unwilling to press the issue until its commercial possibilities had been more clearly established. The Reform party were much more uncomfortable. They reacted to the Intercolonial rather the way the Liberals from Ontario did to the Canadian Pacific Railway some twenty years later, if anything more strongly. The Intercolonial Railway promised little for Canada West; the manufacturing of Canada West had not yet developed to the point of perceiving substantial markets in the Maritime colonies, despite the fact that within a decade it was clear the market *was* there all the time. To the Reform party, the Intercolonial was just another Grand Trunk job, worse in fact, for it promised almost nothing immediate or direct for Canada West except increased taxation to pay for it.

As for the Northwest, here again party attitudes differed. The Reform party, strong in the counties west of Toronto, felt the pull of the Northwest, and looked eagerly to the possibilities of expansion there. Red River had more meaning to the Reform party than the Saint John River did. Thus federation of the Canadas had in it the idea of Canadian annexation of the Northwest, or to put it more accurately perhaps, Canada West's annexation of the Northwest. The Conservative party took the sharper and perhaps the more sensible view that for the moment the Northwest was a white elephant. It would be more trouble, expense, and inconvenience than it was worth. If the Northwest were to be given to the Province of Canada without any expense or effort on Canada's part, it would probably have to be accepted. But the Conservative party's instinct seems to have been to leave the Northwest alone, but to find out more about it by sending out small, energetic expeditions in 1857 and in 1858. What was to make this policy increasingly unenterprising was the growth of the American Northwest, and its concomitant ambitions, represented so graphically by Minnesota's entry as a full state into the American union in 1858.

Broadly speaking, it can be said that Canada East wanted to keep the union of the Province of Canada intact. French Canadians on the Conservative side of politics believed that the Canadian union should be kept going and deplored the sectional, divisive issues raised by Canada West. Nor did French-Canadian Conservatives want dissolution of the Union; they preferred the *status quo*, but if pressed into a change, they were willing to consider Confederation. Not a few French-Canadian Conservatives and most English-Canadian Conservatives in Canada East were committed to the trade and business enterprise that Montreal and its communications with Canada West represented. Confederation also promised the Intercolonial Railway, and thus a still larger range for the metropolitan grasp of Montreal.

On the other hand, the Rouges recognized, as early as 1856, that some adjustments might have to be made, sooner or later, to the Canadian constitution, in order to meet the grievances of Canada West. They were not interested in Confederation of British North America. There were too many unknowns in it. They wanted mainly some internal adjustment in the constitution of the Province of Canada, suggested by the idea of a federal system within the province. Like their English Liberal colleagues in Canada East, as well as their Reform colleagues in Canada West, the Rouges distrusted the Intercolonial Railway project. It would be another Grand Trunk "job" for the Conservative party, without doing much good for trade.

This partly explains the curious history of the Sandfield Macdonald ministry of 1862-64 on the Intercolonial Railway issue. Sandfield Macdonald, the Premier, wanted the Intercolonial — or said he did; but many of his colleagues in the ministry, both from Canada West and from Canada East did not. A. A. Dorion did not. Dorion was in and out of Sandfield Macdonald's government, pretty much according to the state of the Intercolonial Railway issue. Dorion's return to that government, in January, 1863, almost certainly meant that any agreement made with the Maritime provinces at Quebec in September, 1862 on the Intercolonial Railway would be jettisoned if possible. This, in turn, was to bring fierce recriminations from the Maritime colonies when they learned of it finally in September, 1863.

Canadian Politics and the Need for Political Change, 1856-1859

28 OPINIONS ON FEDERAL UNION

Gazette, Montreal
Saturday, April 26, 1856

"He [Brown] has thundered away against a certain class of evils, and in favour of certain reforms, until he has come to consider them the sum total of political good . . . but in appealing to the prejudices of Upper Canadians, has but roused the prejudices of Lower Canadians against him. He has imperilled the existence of the Union by arraying the two sections in open hostility. . . . I am glad to hear, however, that as the cry of dis-Union grows louder, the merits of a Federal Union of British North America are being fully discussed, and men seem fast coming to the belief that that Union is not far distant. While men feel more and more the difficulties of dealing with local questions in a United Parliament, few or none seem willing to give up the hope of founding here, apart from the United States, a Northern nationality for ourselves. While patriots must deplore then the sectionalism which threatens to rend Canada asunder, they may rejoice if, out of so great an evil, so great a good as a Federal Union is to be educed."

29 UNION OF THE COLONIES FROM A NATIONAL VIEWPOINT

La Patrie, Montreal
Monday, November 3, 1856 [translation]

"In the *Acadian Recorder* of last October 11 and 18 we find two note-worthy articles on the subject of the union of the colonies of British North America. These articles attracted our attention and we felt obliged to translate them so as to show our readers in Lower Canada how politicians in Nova Scotia view and treat this important question."

30 FEDERATION OR CLOSER UNION OF THE CANADAS?

Le Pays, Montreal
Saturday, February 7, 1857 [translation]

"Do we have to perpetuate, consolidate the union between Upper and Lower Canada, or has the time come for us to look for 'another form of political existence'? . . . Up to now, in effect, in spite of the legislative union proclaimed in the statute book, each section of the province [of United Canada] has had its own laws, its own ministers, its own political parties, in a word — its own government.

"[But the cry for representation by population will get stronger and it is necessary to recognize this fact.] . . . The time has come, if not already passed, to choose between a complete merging of interests and origins [within the Union] and a profound alteration of our relations with the other British colonies of North America. . . . The repeal of the union has always seemed to us to be the wisest course, but if the people of Lower Canada persist in maintaining it despite everything, we are ready to follow their lead and to swallow our portion of the bitter cup in store."

31 FEDERAL UNION: THE POLITICIAN'S GAME?

Daily Colonist, Toronto
Tuesday, September 22, 1857

" . . . Whenever any difficulty arises between the government and the

43

people, a federal union seems to be the life boat adopted by all sinking statesmen. . . . But whenever present difficulties are got over or rather as soon as a distinct majority can be counted upon in Parliament in favour of the Ministry of the day, the federal union question is hung up to dry, and we hear no more of it till statesmen are in distress again, or till some new sham is necessary to cover over old corruptions."

32 CONCERNING THE NORTH AMERICAN PROVINCES AND FEDERAL UNION

The Quebec *Le Courrier du Canada* began February 2, 1857, under the editorship of Hector Langevin and J. C. Taché, Langevin's name appears for the last time on July 6, 1857, and the next day there began J. C. Taché's series of 33 articles in favour of Confederation of British North America, and which continued intermittently until October 23. They were subsequently published as a booklet in 1858 under the title *Des provinces de l'Amérique du Nord et d'une union fédérale*. The quotations below are cited from the booklet. [translation]

[Taché proposed a federal system whereby the provincial governments would have all powers except the following reserved to the federal government: commerce; central banks; money; weights and measures; customs; public works such as canals, railways, telegraphs, post office; militia; criminal law. He goes on:]
"Each province would thus be in a position to give itself the constitution best suited to itself, without fear of seeing itself forced later on to change it as a result of a separation between the British Empire and the North American Confederation." [p.155-6]
"The federal agreement would rest on the principle of a perpetual and unalterable surrender of powers from the separate governments to the central government within the context of clear spheres of competence established by means of a written constitution." [p.241]

33 CONFEDERATION OF THE PROVINCES

La Patrie, Montreal
Saturday, October 17, 1857 [translation]

"Almost all great questions spring from the political life of nations in the unforeseen and sudden way that marks each of the great dates of history.
"It is not that these events lack painstaking preparation; on the contrary the work toward them has gone on gradually, by itself so to speak, so that it proceeded unnoticed and its results in consequence cause surprise. . . . For us Lower Canadians a more serious question is at hand, one we scarcely need to point out: in the union of two or three groups of now distinct populations, we should play a role corresponding not only to our numbers but also to our unique position in the centre of population groups around us. . . .An agreement that in respecting the rights of our race, linked us in another way to more general and more numerous groups elsewhere would be, we are sure, welcomed by all; but it does not appear that at this moment our French-Canadian government has anything to gain in a mixture of interests whose long-term advantages can only be anticipated much later on."

34 CONFEDERATION: CANADA AT THE CROSSROADS

Gazette, Montreal
Saturday, April 17, 1858

"We have now in Canada a veritable constitutional crisis replacing the half dozen pretences which have passed away. The pressure for representation by population contemporaneously with a loudly reiterated demand . . . for the preservation of the double majority system . . . produces a new issue, which now or shortly hereafter must be tried and decided. Shall we draw closer the present Legislative Union; or shall we relax it in favour of the principle of federation, so as to enable us to add new territories from time to time, taken from the Colonies of the East or the unorganized Territories of the West? It is in this broader aspect we hope to see Parliament deal with the much vexed question now before it. . . . If the Federal principle is insisted upon by French Canadians, British Canadians should urge its extension. If we are never to have thorough legislative union of the two parts of Canada . . . better begin immediately to fashion the framework of a larger confederation. . . . If Montreal and the Eastern Townships are not willing to be governed by the Peninsula of Upper Canada, they are not altogether delighted with the prospect of entire submission to Three Rivers, Quebec, or Gaspé . . . a central Province comprising that part of Canada east of the Bay of Quinte and west of the eastern boundary of the Eastern Townships comprising the river (St. Lawrence and Ottawa) counties in Upper Canada, Montreal and the Eastern townships in the Lower, must come about. The East may stand still as long as it likes; the West rush as frantically onward: this great central district is that part of Canada where the speedy assimilation and codification of the laws, progress in commerce and manufactures, lumbering and mining, that gradual, sure, true progress which is the best indication of material prosperity, may be most certainly looked for."

35 THE IMPRACTICABLE DOUBLE MAJORITY

Daily Colonist, Toronto
Saturday, May 22, 1858

" . . . the people of Canada have no relish for abstractions. In all their thoughts and ways they are essentially a hard-headed, business, unimaginative people; and an orator more potent by far than Mr. Cauchon would signally fail who should address himself to topics having no obvious, no real, relationship to the material concerns of the day. Now the double majority doctrine comes within this category. It is just about as practical and important as Godwin's doctrine of human perfectibility, and has about the same relationship to the feelings of the Canadian public. . . . The community, as such, cares not one jot about the question; and the result will remain the same, though zealots from Lower Canada, and tricksters from Lower Canada, talk till the crack of doom. Something more vivid than perverted references to musty precedent, and more honest than the confessions of statesmen of the Howland calibre, will be required to produce any different effect."

36 BY WHAT POLICY ARE WE TO BE GOVERNED?

Daily Colonist, Toronto
Wednesday, June 30, 1858

This editorial, from the pen of George Sheppard, marks the *Colonist's* break with the Conservative party of Cartier and Macdonald.

"Parliament has been four months in session, and where are its results? . . . By what policy are we to be governed? By what principles are we to be guided? To whom shall we look for the measures that are needed to save the country from ruin?

"These are questions which demand, and must have, an answer. The public have waited expectantly and most patiently, until the time for forbearance is ended. . . .

"Whether Mr. Macdonald or Mr. Brown shall be Premier, may be the vital question which we have been trying to believe it is. Whether Mr. Cayley shall remain the administrator of the financial affairs for the Province, may be a problem surpassing in importance the general welfare of the industrial and mercantile interests that now lie gasping for existence. But we confess that to our poor judgement these personal considerations have lost much of their significance. . . .

"The ground upon which the Moderate party justified its claims to electoral support, was its professed readiness and ability to inaugurate a policy suited to the times. Yet, to this hour, we are without, not merely a policy, but the faintest resemblance to anything of the kind. . . . the 'policy' of the session has been simply a series of quirks and quibbles. . . . "

---

37 SPEECH BY GALT ON CONFEDERATION

Daily Colonist, Toronto
Tuesday, July 6, 1858

A report of the debates on July 5. Galt is speaking on the Representation by Population question posed by Cameron and as amended with 3 months hoist by Cauchon.

If government had brought in a federation proposal, said Galt, "Their position, instead of growing daily weaker would have been infinitely stronger, and they would not have found the opposition accumulating against them. — How were we to expect to control the great western territory, unless we established a system of local self-government? Here was half of a mighty continent offered to them. If they were to take it how was it proposed to govern it? Would a simple land agent be sufficient? No, inducements must be held out to the ambitions of those who settled there. In the United States, if people went to one of their territories, there was the prospect before them of taking part in their own government — of being governors, legislators or judges. . . . He desired to come before the House as the advocate of the confederation of the whole of the British Provinces of North America. He desired to see all their energies directed into one channel, and under one control, for then, he believed they would achieve a great future. The people here desired to be no longer a Province, but to become a nation. There must be the national policy inaugurated. The Imperial Government offered no obstruction; they wished to concede what the colonists desired. . . . Every member in the House must be aware of the position of the Provinces. Each of them were absorbed in its own resources, — attending to its own interests. Almost the first we had heard of Newfoundland was when its people thought they were going to be delivered over, bound hand and foot, by the treaty with France. This showed that the interests of the Provinces, treated in detail must be sacrificed. Would such be possible with 3,000,000 of people represented on the floor of one House? We saw the deference which was paid to us in Canada, even now — two Provinces being united. How much would not this be increased if the whole, like a bundle of sticks, were bound together? He would be glad of an opportunity of going into the discussion of the manner in which the scheme of a federal government should be carried out, but he would not now do so, further than to say that there must be one general government to attend to the general interest, such as the control of public works, of banks, post offices, lighthouses, harbors, provisional government for the western territory. Local legislature would have the control of local objects. In proposing a federal system, he by no means thought the American one should be adopted — we might copy that in its good points and avoid its defects, and at the same time preserve the flexibility of our own constitution. Of course in any change which migh [sic] be proposed, he did not think any difficulty would arise with the mother country. The source of Canada's weakness was her long exposed frontier. If the colonies were united, we would have a bulwark to the east, and would not be required in the event of disorder to form a constitution or to enter into treaties the one colony with the other."

---

38 COMMENT ON GALT'S SPEECH

Leader, Toronto
Tuesday, July 6, 1858

A leading Conservative newspaper in Toronto makes light of Galt's Confederation proposal, very much, indeed, as the Conservative government itself did.

"Mr. Galt had a great bundle of notes before him; from which he delivered a speech containing a superfluity of prelude. The scheme and the facts were long in coming; and when they did come, it was easy to see that they excited no enthusiasm and were hardly able to engage the serious attention of the House. . . . We have no hesitation in saying that no government could have made the Federal Union project a Cabinet question. The little interest which Mr. Galt's eloquence excited should have sufficed to convince him of this; and indeed he seems not to have been wholly unconscious of it, for he let fall the sxpression [sic] that he probably stood alone in the House, in the position he had taken, and he preferred not to test the popularity of the scheme in the House by moving an amendment. . . . A revolution of so pretentious a character as that whieh [sic] he proposes cannot be made all at once. It must be preceded by years of discussion. Mr. Galt last night made the first speech probably ever made, in the legislature, in favor of the scheme . . . . Should the chances of political fortune make Mr. Galt minister four or five years hence, he will find it quite soon enough to make the project of a federal union a cabinet question."

---

39 UPPER CANADA AND FEDERATION: INDECISION OF THE GOVERNMENT

Daily Colonist, Toronto
Tuesday, July 6, 1858

"The members of the Government last night followed their usual course in dealing with the question of the Federation of the Colonies, raised by Mr. Galt. Not one of them dared to meet the issue raised. . . . The Premier [John A. Macdonald] had not a word to say on the question of policy; his single aim was to evade it. Mr. McGee hit the ruling feature of the Ministerial course, which is to get over each succeeding week of the session as best they can, and to be religiously thankful when Sunday comes to relieve them from chances of defeat. Mr. Cartier alone mustered pluck to speak; and certainly he shrieked to perfection. It was a pitiful hit, most appropriate manifestotion [sic] of Ministerial weakness to see the Attorney-General East, — the only spokesman of the Government on the occasion — dodging the questions before the House; dodging the question of Representation by Population, and the question of Federation; and rendering himself ridiculous by uttering oracular and most ignorant statements in reference to the working of the American system of Government. The significance of Federation, as a method of relief amidst the difficulties that now beset the politics of Canada, was felt by every unofficial member; the Government alone,

47

lacking courage or principle to meet matters on their merits, struggled hard to preserve a silence. . . .

"We can understand this course on the part of the Premier: he must be silent or abusive, and abuse will not solve the problem of federation. We can understand Mr. Cayley's silence, for that minister, Heaven knows, is lost in the mazes of the tariff which neither he nor anybody else can reconcile with principle. We can understand Mr. Cartier, who is at best a French-Canadian edition of the terrier breed. But Mr. Sicotte passes comprehension. . . . "

40 FREEDOM OF THE PRESS

Daily Colonist, Toronto
Monday, July 19, 1858

"It is not the fashion in Canadian politics to give or take quarter. . . .We did not commence our hostile criticism upon the Government without being prepared for harsh judgments on our motives, and not over-tender comments on our conduct. It was evident that in severing relations which had been to some extent confidential . . . we exposed ourselves to the animadversions the reverse of friendly, and to a personal malignity which, on the part of the Premier, we had good reason to know was without bounds. Nor have we been disappointed. . . . Having discovered that, in Mr. John A. Macdonald's opinion, newspaper organship is the synonym of newspaper slavery, to be carried on only at the cost of everything like self-respect, we exercised the undoubted right of leaving that individual to find a journal more suited to his patronage; and on the instant we became 'hireling scribes'."

41 WINDS OF CHANGE NEEDED

Daily Colonist, Toronto
Monday, August 2, 1858

"We may change our Government as often as we please; but unless there is an important change made in the constitution of the country, the whole thing will be the farce it has been for years past. The very first step in the formation of a Cabinet is demoralizing. So many sections have to be propitiated — so much has to be promised with the view of securing The Parliamentary majority — that men who go into power with perfectly clean hands, get into the mire at the very outset of their ministerial career. . . .

"The history of the last four years proves all this. And it is not that our public men are so much more corrupt than those of other countries enjoying popular government: it is simply that we have a bad system — a system entirely unsuited to the condition and character of the people. The British system, excellent as it unquestionably is, as applied to the mother country, is sadly brought into disrepute here; and no one will seriously affirm that it can continue for a very long time.

"The public departments are neglected because the Ministers are overwhelmed with legislative duty and party manoeuvring. . . . A Federal Union, which, of course, is the only solution any new Government can have to offer for the question of Representation, will be the first step toward a new state of things. But we cannot avow any very strong hopes in the ability of the class of politicians generally at present on the stage to bring matters to a satisfactory issue. To hold, however, the reins of Government at all, they must make a venture on some important changes in the system. And every one who has any public spirit, will wish them not to make a mess of it."

42 GALT'S VISION OF A UNITED CANADA

Pilot, Montreal
Thursday, August 19, 1858

Galt's address in Sherbrooke on Federal Union.

Galt notes the position of the Hudson's Bay Company territory, "comprising, it is said, one of the finest portions of the Continent, and which are now, on the Pacific coasts, brought into prominent notice, by the discoveries of the Fraser Gold Fields. . . . To bring them under the same system of Government, to open these fertile plains to the enterprize of our people, is a most important subject; but it is difficult to see how it can be done, under our present constitution. . . . it is plainly the duty of Canada, to take the initiative in the consideration of the question of a Federal Union. . . . So far as my own private judgment goes, I cannot see any other escape from existing difficulties. Temporary expedients might be resorted to, . . . but the germ of evil and discontent would remain, ready to break out at any moment. Much better then, is it, to enquire, whether we can finally dispose of all sources of local discontent, and find in the diversities of race, and religion, an incentive to honourable rivalry in favor of our common country, rather than to leave them, as now, the subjects by which any party leader may build upon evanescent and baneful popularity, by arraying one class against another. For my own part, I look forward with a sanguine hope to the day when our statesmen will have longer and nobler objects of ambition, and when the care of the extended interests of a confederation, embracing the whole British Possessions in North America, will obscure those purely sectional views, which unhappily have now too great prominence."

43 CONFEDERATION AND THE PEOPLE: FICKLENESS OF THE PUBLIC

Daily Colonist, Toronto
Tuesday, August 31, 1858

"'The future of Canada' — 'The destinies of Canada' — 'The development of the resources of the country' — such are the tinkling cymbals with whose incessant din the public ear is tickled. But does the thinking portion of the community believe that the noisy enunciation of stale platitudes will ensure the glorious destiny they are thus taught to dream of? Will sensible men rely for the consummation of this anticipated future upon the hyperbole of the ranting demagogue? Will they not rather put their trust in the honest energy of the tried and faithful advocate? Assuredly they will; but the world is not all so sensible as it is prone to fancy itself. Reflection is not the grand characteristic of the crowd. The many love ease, mental ease especially. . . .

"From the commencement of her political history, Canada has been remarkable for what may be termed the consumption of public men. . . . Our leading men pass away like phantoms. They are no sooner fairly launched than the tide of popular favor begins to ebb. The names of Viger, Papineau, Blake, Baldwin, Lafontaine, Hincks, MacNab are only some among those whom a very few years have seen go [out?] of the arena of public life."

44 A FEDERAL UNION: ITS NATURE, FORM AND CONSEQUENCES

British Colonist, Toronto
Tuesday, October 26, 1858

This editorial was also copied by the Halifax *British Colonist*, November 9, 1858.

"What is commonly understood by a federal union is that which is familiar to and existing amoung [sic] our southern neighbours. . . . Such an union worked in the British Provinces would give a local government and local Parliament to each while one general Parliament and one general government would be a contribution from all, intended as the central power of the whole union. What might be the power each Province would choose to delegate to the central government it is· not just now necessary to inquire. . . .

"There is a kind of union, however, distinct from this, with which Canadians are more directly conversant — legislative union of the two Provinces. Notwithstanding our familiarity with this latter mode, there seems to be but one conception as to that which is to be followed in any new connexion with the sister Provinces — that of a pure and simple confederacy. None other appears to have been in any way contemplated.

"There are, at the present moment, many unmistakeable indications that the existing relative positions of the British North America Colonies towards each other, and it may be towards the rest of the world also, are rapidly approaching a state of change. A subject in which upwards of three millions of people are so deeply interested as their own nationality is not likely, after many years of debate, to be abandoned without results. . . . "

Three or four years ago the question was discussed in reference to Canada, Nova Scotia, New Brunswick and Prince Edward Island. "Now our aspirations have a higher range, and the vista includes the Hudson's Bay territory, the vast prairies of the Northwest, and ends nothing short of the Fraser river and the shores of the Pacific. The contemplation of such an union, or rather the establishment of one homogenous government over so large a country, changes the entire aspect of the whole issue." The Maritime provinces could not effect such a union and " . . . the prompt agency of Canadian statesmanship is indispensable. We trust when the time for action does arrive, the subject will be dealt with in no peddling spirit — that the dirty jobbery and political scoundrelism, which has made Canada a byword, will not be found to taint the councils which will direct this great work to a fitting consummation."

The legislative union of the Canadas has and "undoubtedly offers the greater facility for the immediate assumption of a sovereignty. . . . A general government will always be more powerful than that which is merely central and possessing only a limited authority.

"The chief objection to a legislative union has been based on the geographical position of members of the union. This objection might have been urged with some reason before the construction of railroads but every year is detracting from its force. Within the space which will be found necessary for the adjustment of a confederation, it is highly probable that every mile of the road from Halifax to Lake Superior will be travelled by rail . . . there are, on the other hand, reasons which render a federal organization popular. The strongest is to be found in the desire to retain as large an amount of self-government as is compatible with confederated membership. It should not be forgotten, however, that natural and even just as this may be, it will necessarily enfeeble the central government. This predilection, if an obstacle to a more preferable form, might, perhaps, be met by the application of uniform municipal institutions . . .

"We have raised the question of a

legislative, as opposed to a federal union, for the purpose of attracting public attention to them rather than advocating the merits of either. Our impression is that the general public has hitherto entertained no distinction respecting the specific character of the contemplated union. This distinction however is becoming daily of more and more importance . . . the character of the union becomes a first and vital consideration — it may be the creation of a political chaos, or the foundations of an empire."

45 LOWER CANADA AND UNION: VIEW OF THE MINORITY

Mercury, Quebec
Saturday, May 28, 1859

"Not only is the existing Union prejudicial to all Lower Canadian interests, but more especially to the interests of Lower Canadian Protestants. For them the present Union is an Egyptian bondage, its dissolution would be a political millenium. . . . Upper Canada uniformly recognizes Lower Canada in its majority alone, its minority it as uniformly ignores. . . . Every middle aged man in the country remembers the past glory, contrasts it with the present degradation of the British party, and regards the Act of Union as the fountain from which their degradation has been derived."

46 LOWER CANADA AND UNION: NEED FOR CONSTITUTIONAL CHANGE

Transcript, Montreal
Thursday, July ,14, 1859

"We are not a homogeneous people. . . . We find now no greater fusion or blending of feeling and interest than at the commencement of the experiment.

In all matters of legislation and government, the French seek to advance their own interests, without any care for Upper Canada, and the British of Upper Canada, in like manner, study what will be of benefit, not of the whole Province, but of their own section of it. The Executive, subjected to constant pressure from these opposing forces, are placed in circumstances of extreme difficulty. . . . We do not see how, on the survey of the history of the past eighteen years, the conclusion can be avoided that some change in our constitutional system must be made, in order to save Canada from going further on the downward career to helpless embarrassment."

Opposition to Confederation and Support for the Federation of the Two Canadas, 1857-1860

47 A UNION OF THE BRITISH AMERICAN COLONIES

Stratford Beacon, Stratford
Friday, August 21, 1857

"Much has lately been said in favor of a legislative union of the British American Colonies and it has been asserted that the locality to be selected as the seat of government will be decided upon with a view to such an event. We never could see what Canada would gain by an union with New Brunswick, Nova Scotia, or Newfoundland, which she has not now. . . . In the proposed union, we cannot discover whether it is intended that each colony shall possess a legislature of its own, or whether the legislative powers will all be vested in the legislature which shall be composed of representatives from the countries in question. . . . When the Honorable Joseph Howe, of Nova Scotia, first mooted the idea of a legislative union of the British American Colonies, it was then as much regarded as utopian as at present; but a freshness has been thrown around the discussion by the lectures which Judge Haliburton, of Nova Scotia, has been delivering in England and Scotland, and more recently by an article which appeared . . . . in a late issue of *Blackwood's Magazine*. . . . The politicians of Nova Scotia and New Brunswick are shrewd enough to see that Upper Canada is a fat goose, and they no doubt sincerely wish to step in to help Lower Canada to fleece her. What an easy matter it would be for the corruptionists of these colonies — Lower Canada included of course — to put their heads together and vote to spend our money in their respective sections!"

---

48 CONFEDERATION: WHAT ARE ITS ADVANTAGES?

Weekly Herald, Montreal
Saturday, May 8, 1858

"We expect to hear a detailed enumeration of thousands of square miles, and the millions of square acres embraced within the Nova Scotian and New Brunswick boundaries . . . we shall have the usual flourishes with which, on this continent, one sets off his descriptions of wild lands, whether they be situated on the fever swamps of Illinois or the frozen regions of the Saguenay. . . . Then the coast line will be traced up and down the two shores of the Bay of Fundy, round by Canso and old Louisbourg, till we get again to our own territory a little this side of the Bay of Chaleurs, from whence we shall be asked to travel through the Straits of Northumberland, taking a view of the mackerel and herring grounds there and in the Bras d'Or; and having thus circumnavigated St. Johns [*i.e.*, P.E.I.] and Cape Breton, we shall probably be invited to dine on cod in Newfoundland, which, being an outlying possession, will be treated in a detached manner. We shall hear of the 'noble' forests of these countries; the statistics of their shipbuilding will be spread out in unimpeachable and imposing tabular statements; the mines will come in for their share of the general panegyric, and there will be thrown in a sketch of all the people who have thriven by the fishing business from the Ichthyosauri, who lived upon fish because they could get nothing else. . . . But having looked at and admired all the provisions which Providence has made for the maintenance of a large population around the Gulf of St. Lawrence, the question will yet have to be answered — how will confederation make these resources any more our own then they are at this moment? . . . We shall have a federal legislature ten times more extravagant than the present, and committing ten times more jobs; and we shall have another edition of the Grand Trunk Railway, with this difference, that the extravagance and bad management of the road we have, at least procured something that was wanted, while the new railroad will pass where no one wants to go. In the first Grand Trunk the railroad was made for the country. In the second an imaginary railroad wants a country and we are asked to make one for it, as our industrious grandmothers used to make their quilts — by patchwork."

---

49 OPPOSITION TO THE INTERCOLONIAL RAILROAD

Globe, Toronto
Friday, October 8, 1858

The following editorial was also quoted by the Saint John *Morning News,* October 22, 1858.

"The commercial advantages to be derived from a union of the Lower Provinces are hardly appreciable, while in the boundless west there lies open to us a field of enterprise which might cause wealth to flow into every city and village of our land. Why should Canada, at this moment, spend any portion of her means in building a road to Halifax? She will not thereby raise the price of a barrel of flour a single cent, nor will she find in the Lower Provinces a market for any of her manufactures. As an outlet to the ocean, this intercolonial railroad is a mere farce. No one able to take ship at Portland [Maine] or Quebec, would ever dream of travelling by railway to Halifax. And yet this work will engage four or five millions [£] of capital . . . . If the Imperial Government is willing to grant assistance for the development of British power in North America, let her grant it in aid of the Pacific Railway. . . . Let her expend it in founding a great colony on Lake Winnipeg and the Saskatchewan."

50 WHAT WOULD A FEDERATION ACCOMPLISH?

London Free Press, London
Thursday, November 11, 1858

A Reform newspaper puts the Conservative government's espousal of Confederation as merely a question of political convenience.

"Very little faith seems to be put by the public in the cry for Federation of the Provinces, which has been raised by some of those who are afraid to grapple with present difficulties, and are willing to start any new question or idea in order to avoid the unpleasant duty of dealing with immediate necessities. At present, the subject can only be treated as an abstract one, and in that light it is an Imperial far more than a Colonial one. It may be that Imperial policy would be advanced by the erection of a number of colonies on the American continent, but of what benefit to Canada we have not at present seen well defined. . . . It is questionable, therefore, whether it would be at all useful for Canada to enter into an expensive political alliance with distant countries — though sister colonies — when the commercial interests are so slender as to be represented by a sum which is insufficient to denominate the business done in a fourth-rate Canadian town. Nor has the little amount of commercial intercourse which has occurred, increased during the last four years to any marked extent. In 1854, the imports from the four colonies were set down at £168,778, and those of last year exceeded them by but something less than £20,000. Commercial relations as between Canada and the Atlantic Colonies are thus insignificant indeed . . . . So far, then, as Canada is concerned [what with the increase in cost of a Federal system], but little practical benefit seems likely to accrue from the Federation sought. The game would not be worth the candle! . . . The reason why the question is agitated just now by the ministerial press is quite palpable. The attempt is made to distract the public mind from the financial condition of the Province, and engage it in vain-glorious aspirations after empire. It is in the same principle that the boat's crew, when pursued by a whale, toss out a tub. This federation is the hollow political tub of the ministry, who find themselves inconveniently pressed by public opinion. . . . Meanwhile, we trust that the public mind will not be diverted from the necessities of today, in order to contemplate national glories which may be in store for Canada during a future generation. The best foundation upon which a people's happiness can rest is remunerative agriculture, manufactures, trade and commerce, fostered by good laws administered by honest men. To matters such as these, and not to the glories of such schemes as a federation, should the attention of public men be directed."

51 IS A FEDERAL UNION REQUIRED?

London Free Press, London
Thursday, November 25, 1858

"Public opinion seems to be setting very decidedly against the proposition for a Federal Union of the British North American Provinces. . . . We are yet [having cited Saint John New Brunswick *Courier*] but a small and poor people. . . . This longing which exists in some minds to bring the region between the Atlantic and Pacific, lying north of the United States, under Canadian rule, is but of the kind which induced the poor frog . . . to endeavor to assume the proportions of the ox. The result was inevitable; and if a people small in numbers; poor in capital; and living amid still undeveloped resources, attempts to expand suddenly into magnificent proportion, the fate that overtook the silly frog, will inevitably be shared by itself."

52 THE MISSION A FAILURE

Perth Courier, Perth
Friday, November 19, 1858

"This Mission was not undertaken on the ground of promoting a broad national policy, but for the paltry purpose of diverting public attention in Canada from the Seat of Government

and Representation questions, and it therefore deserved no better fate. The British Government and the English capitalists have no faith in the Cartier-Macdonald shufflers, and some other dodge will have to be tried to bolster up the corruptionists. Let the Federation Scheme be undertaken in good faith by honest men, backed up by the honestly expressed opinion of the colonists, and success must attend it; but undertaken by political tricksters as a political dodge, failure is inevitable."

53 THE DEATH OF CONFEDERATION?

Weekly Herald, Montreal
Saturday, February 12, 1859

"It will be seen that the project has fallen as flat in England and in the other Colonies as it did in Parliament, when Mr. Galt, previous to his joining the Ministry, almost failed to get a quorum to hear his views, and when, of course, Mr. Cartier and his then colleagues voted against the plan, which, three weeks after, they announced as their grand stroke of policy for the salvation of Canada. As to the Colonies, Nova Scotia and Prince Edward's Island do not seem to have thought it worth while to reply at all, and New Brunswick declines to have anything to do with it. . . . [As for Newfoundland, the French shore controversy is an ominous indication of] the sort of embroglio into which this precious incorporation of dispersed elements would lead us."

54 FEDERATION: A MEANS OF DEALING WITH LOWER CANADA

Globe, Toronto
Monday, July 11, 1859

"Let there be a strictly federative

union of the two sections of Canada, and we of the West will be relieved from the great source of existing difficulties. Conceding to the French the credit which their political conduct earned before the present union, we are obliged to hold them accountable for many of the anomalies and much of the wrong which now disgrace the system. They have evinced no forbearance, no generosity, no justice, in this legislation under the union. . . . change the nature of the alliance from legislative to federative, and you at once draw the teeth and cut the clans of Lower Canada. . . . Her people will be enabled no more to enjoy money wrung from Upper Canadian labour . . . our preference, therefore, is for 'a scheme of federation for Canada' — a reality, having no resemblance to the ministerial myth."

55 QUO VADIS, O CANADA?

Sarnia Observer, Sarnia
Friday, October 21, 1859

"Some two years ago, the scheme of a Federal Union of the British North American Provinces was proposed by the present Ministry, as the best means of getting rid of the difficulties referred to; and several members of the present Government made a special trip to England for the express purpose of obtaining Imperial sanction to the scheme. The mission failed. It was well known in England that the maritime Provinces of Nova Scotia, New Brunswick, &c., either opposed it or viewed it with indifference, nor did they need any special connection with Canada. . . . after our Ministers returned, the matter was dropped. Previously it had been puffed up as the grand panacea for all the evils arising from difference of race, laws and religion; but after Messrs. Galt, Cartier and Company returned from England, the project, with all its splendid advantages, was allowed to sink into oblivion; and worse than

all, no substitute was proposed in its stead. . . .

"Looking at the occurrences of the past, and of the past two years especially, it has become painfully evident to a large portion of the inhabitants of Upper Canada, that the system now in operation can no longer be continued; that *some change* must take place in the mutual relations of the two sections. Representation by Population was until recently looked upon as *the* panacea for the evils in this connection . . . but no proposition which has been made by the west has been received with so great aversion by the Lower Canadians. . . . The Ministerial Federal Union scheme is out of the question, because that too cannot be obtained. The Lower Provinces do not desire it. . . . The only remedy, in our view, is the dissolution of the present connection, and formation of a federative union between Upper and Lower Canada. . . .

"As to the only other proposition which is hinted at by some — *Annexation!* — it is unnecessary to say a word. Not one in a thousand of our population have the most distant desire for such a change."

56 A BLUEPRINT FOR FEDERATION

Perth Courier, Perth
Friday, November 4, 1859

The following statement, made by the opposition members from Canada East in October, 1859, bears a strong resemblance to the proposals that were to come from the Reform convention in November.

"Your Committee are impressed with the conviction that, whether we consider the present needs or the probable future condition of the country, the true, the statesmanlike solution is to be sought in the substitution of a purely *Federative,* for the present so-called, *Legislative* Union. . . .

"In the distribution of powers between the Local, or State, and the Federal Governments, the controlling and pervading idea should be to delegate to the Federal Government such authority only as would be essential to the objects of the federation; and by necessary consequence to reserve to the Subdivisions powers as ample and varied as possible. The Customs, the Post Office, the Laws concerning Patents and Copyrights, the Currency, and such of the Public Works as are of general interest to the whole Province, would form the chief, if not, the only subjects with which the General Government should be charged; while everything relating to purely Local Improvements, to Education, to the Administration of Justice, to the Militia, to Laws relating to Property, and generally all questions of Local concern, — in fine the power to legislate all matters not specifically devolving on the Federal Government — would be lodged in the Government of the Separate Provinces."

Signed by A. A. Dorion, L.T. Drummond, L. A. Dessaulles, T. D'A. McGee.

57 SPEECH BY SHEPPARD

Globe, Toronto
Friday, November 11, 1859

George Sheppard at the great Reform convention in Toronto, in November, 1859, spoke out against federation of the two Canadas. Instead he urged outright dissolution of the Canadian Union. His argument is telling, although his dissolution amendment was defeated by George Brown.

"The Federative principle had its origin in the United States, with national institutions, national exigencies, and having in view national rather than colonial results. If you say you desire Federation because it would be a great step to a nationality, then I am with you. But if it is to be a Federation, with a view to nationality, let us have a Federation of all the Provinces. . . . [A federation of the Canadas] would be holding up without meaning it, a strong central power, and federation, as we understand it in this country, with a viceroy on top of it, would be found to involve a very expensive government."

58 FEDERATION: THE NEED FOR CLARITY

Globe, Toronto
Saturday, November 12, 1859

George Sheppard speaking to his dissolution amendment (Thursday, November 10), "What are you going to give your Federative Government to do? Are you prepared to create local governments, and then to create a central legislature, a central executive, with a viceroy at the top — all to transact the business of a Province? . . . If you want a principle which shall rouse public attention, it must be a principle which commands itself to the common sense of the community. . . . "

"Do these gentlemen propose that the Federal Government shall control the public lands? Do they propose that the Federal Government, composed equally of Upper and Lower Canadian members shall manage the settlement of land in Upper Canada? (Cheers). I contend, then, that this conflict of opinion on one of the simplest points proves that there are no differences greater between them and me, than there are between the advocates of Federation themselves. Call upon them to tell you the details of their scheme, to show its working, to define the powers which they are willing to confer upon the central government; and at once you discover that no two agree. (Cheers). You may say what you will about the difficulties incident to Dissolution, but there are difficulties a little greater in the way of Federation.

(Renewed Cheers) . . . Do you imagine in Federation the debt is to be transferred to the Federal Government and no question asked? Do you think Upper Canada will give a Federal authority control over that very treasury which has been the source of so much heart-burning — so much extravagance and ruin? . . . You say that Upper Canada is to have preponderance in the federation. What does the federative principle rest upon, if not on an equality of rights, an equality of powers? . . . Is federation proposed because it is a step toward nationality? If so, I can imagine thousands who would bear the extra expense on that ground. But let it be avowed beforehand, that we may know what we are about. Say that your federation is with a view to nationality, and I am with you; not otherwise. (Applause.)"

59 BROWN AND FEDERATION

Globe, Toronto
Wednesday, November 16, 1859

Brown's speech carried the Reform convention on the principle of federation of the Canadas by an overwhelming majority.

"But I think it clearly evident that the scheme of the Committee carries with it all the advantages of dissolution, without its disadvantages. What is it that has most galled the people of Upper Canada in the working of the existing Union? Has it not been the injustice done to Upper Canada in local and sectional matters? Has it not been the expenditure of Provincial funds for local purposes of Lower Canada which here are defrayed from local taxation? Has it not been the control exercised by Lower Canada over matters purely pertaining to Upper Canada — the framing of our School laws, the selection of our ministers, the appointment of our local officials? Has it not been that the minority of Upper Canada rule here through Lower Canada votes — that extravagant expenditures are voted by men who have not to provide the means — that fresh taxes are continually imposed by those who have not to pay them? (Cheers)." The Committee's plan strikes at all these grievances. Local and sectional matters will be left to the local governments and general matters given to the general government. "And the matters assigned to the general government are to be clearly defined — not left to doubt, not left open to future encroachment . . . .

"Now, Sir, I do place the question [of federation] on the ground of nationality. I do hope there is not one Canadian in this assembly who does not look forward with high hope to the day when these northern countries shall stand out among the nations of the world as one great confederation. (Cheers). What true Canadian can witness the tide of immigration now commencing to flow into the vast territories of the North-West without longing to have a share in the first settlement of that great and fertile country — who does not feel that to us rightfully belongs the right and the duty of carrying the blessings of civilization throughout those boundless regions, and making our own country the highway of traffic to the Pacific? (Cheers)."

60 THE CHOICES FACING THE COLONIES

Transcript, Montreal
Tuesday, November 15, 1859

"Some thought that a written constitution would act as an efficient check on the proclivities of men in power to extravagance and corruption; others favoured a dissolution pure and simple of the Union between the two Canadas, each Province being likely to manage its own affairs . . . more economically . . . than under the present system, which tempts Lower Canadian representatives to grab all they can for Lower Canada purposes, and Upper Canadian representatives to grab all they can for Upper Canada purposes — each member of the partnership helping to bankrupt the common firm by a greedy appropriation to itself of all it can clutch out of the common purse. By another and more numerous class, the substitution of a Federative for the present Legislative Union was advocated as the most satisfactory remedy. A few urged a Federation of all the British American Provinces; and a small section of the Upper Canada Reformers were in favour of still continuing the struggle for Representation by Population, which had been given up by the leaders of the party as unattainable."

61 LACK OF OBSTACLES TO FEDERATION

Globe, Toronto
Friday, November 25, 1859

"And if that [Mr. Galt's scheme] has failed, if the Lower Provinces have rejected his proffers, what possible objection can they now make to Canadian federation. If the federative plan was good for the whole North American Provinces, it is surely good for the Canadas and the North West. It cannot be alleged that the country is too confined, for Nova Scotia and New Brunswick would add a very small proportion to its area. It cannot be alleged that the population is too limited because it is more than three-fourths of the whole. Is there anything in striking off a fourth of the population which destroys the federative principle?"

62 THE PRICE OF PROVINCIALISM

Stratford Beacon, Stratford
Friday, December 2, 1859

"Often do we read of 'Halifax, Nova Scotia,' but the Canadian public are not yet favoured with a Canadian map of the Lower Provinces and of Canada, with the British possessions to and towards the North Pole. We have to rely on the 'peddled' maps published in the United States. . . . "

63 FRENCH-CANADIAN PESSIMISM OVER CONFEDERATION

L'Ordre, Montreal
Friday, May 4, 1860 [translation]

"What French Canadian has not in his heart cursed a hundred times the Union of the two Canadas? . . . Others have wanted in turn to *anglicize* us and *protestantize* us: after a century of ignoble hopes and base efforts, convinced of their failure, they now want to destroy our constitution. . . . This is what Mr. Brown requested in his speech of last Monday on the constitutional reforms necessitated by a combination of circumstances that human wisdom could not otherwise overcome . . . . [While it is true Upper Canada has paid more money in taxes than Lower Canada, who has helped to pay Upper Canadian debts?] What would Upper Canada be today without the Union? Nothing more or less than a forest put up for auction by British capitalists to repay their investments."

[The only solution is repeal of the Union. Upper Canada does not like living with us: we like it still less.]

58

64 INCONSISTENCY OF THE GOVERNMENT TOWARD FEDERATION

Weekly Herald, Montreal
Saturday, May 26, 1860

"[The] leaders of the party now in the ascendancy, who two years ago reconstructed their Ministry on the basis of Mr. Galt's declarations in Parliament, that some change of an organic nature was required, have now made an opposite statement. They who lately avowed it a part of their policy henceforth to labour for the formation of a confederacy of the whole of the British North American Provinces, have now not only ceased to move toward the promotion of their own remedy for evils which they officially recognized as grave and imminent, but they have voted against a recognition of the same ills as requiring redress. . . .

"[During] the present session the same Parliament, under the same leadership, which informed to Imperial authorities that some great change was required, and who sent home able negotiators to urge that change, have now authoritatively informed us that we live in the best possible world, where any change would be for the worse, and where it is a pious and patriotic duty to keep things just as they are. Of course the different projects of the Upper Canadian minority have been voted down."

65 FEDERATION: THE GREAT UNKNOWN

Transcript, Montreal
Saturday, November 10, 1860

"Humbug! — The *Quebec Chronicle* says 'Federation is the great question of the hour,' when not a human being troubles himself about the question. No province has declared itself in favour of Federation. The Canadian Parliament has not uttered a voice in its favour, and when Canadian Ministers gave an obiter dictum in favour of a scheme, resting on their own incapacity to carry out the government of this country, not a single Province of British North America responded to the call. Canada, with such a government as it now possesses, . . . offers no inducements for its alliance. Not a single North American Province would vote for it."

Shallows of the Early 'Sixties, the Intercolonial Railway, and the Northwest

66 SUPPORT FOR THE CREATION OF THE NORTHWEST INTO A SEPARATE COLONY

Leader, Toronto
Friday, January 27, 1860

Canada should not annex the Northwest, despite what the *Globe* urges. The *Leader's* editorial was quoted by the Red River *Nor'Wester,* March 28, 1860.

"Annexation and federation are, in this case, antagonistic ideas. . . . a little reflection would serve to show that the great North-west can never be governed by a central government of which the seat would have to be on the banks of the Ottawa. A federal government would get rid of the whole difficulty; but in the meantime it is desirable that Red River should be organized into a separate colony, preparatory to its entrance into the family of federated Provinces."

67 A PRESCIENT FORECAST OF THE COALITION OF 1864

London Free Press, London
Wednesday, June 6, 1860

"A National Party, which will seek to place Canada upon a footing worthy of her, and endeavor to consolidate its interests rather than to split them up and weaken them, will have its rise in the fusion [of parties] we alluded to, let it come when it may. For there are but two courses for Canadians to take; the one to promote Canadianism as a national principle, or, to be content to allow the Province to lapse into the confederation of the United States. . . . "

68 GROWING PRESSURE TO DEAL WITH THE QUESTION OF FEDERATION

Gazette, Montreal
Monday, November 19, 1860

The *Gazette* is commenting on P. S. Hamilton's pamphlet, *Letter to His Grace the Duke of Newcastle, upon a Union of the Colonies of British North America* (Halifax, 1860), first published in the Halifax *Acadian Recorder,* October 27, 1860.

"Since the action taken upon Mr. Galt's resolutions [of 1858] and Sir Edmund Head's despatches, nothing seems to have been done anywhere to promote the union, except the occasional discussion of the topic by the colonial press. But the time is clearly enough approaching in Canada when it must enter directly into our politics, as an element of first importance. . . . The partnership now existing between the two portions of Canada can only be maintained by mutual concessions and a national policy. . . . "

69 LOWER CANADA AND FEDERATION

L'Ordre, Montreal
Monday, March 11, 1861 [translation]

"It is not without surprise nor some sorrow that we see the *Canadien* [of Quebec City] recently calling with all its heart and mind for the confederation of the North American provinces . . . . Does this cowardly cry, a prelude to suicide, really come from our heart? An immoral confederation plan, with a constitution the first clause of which would emphasise the utter insignificance of our influence . . . ? Confederation! It will happen if the French-Canadian people remain ignorant of its own interests, its duty and its rights."

[The only condition on which it might be acceptable would be if the Union Act were repealed and a Lower Canadian parliament would be able to discuss conditions.]

Friday, March 22, 1861 [translation]

"We want no part of a confederation patched up in England, made without consulting the French-Canadian people . . . . but if ever growing political difficulties make that form of government absolutely necessary. . . . we would ask that it be brought about in the least harmful manner. . . . "

70 FRENCH-CANADIAN SUPPORT FOR THE INTERCOLONIAL RAILWAY

La Minerve, Montreal
Tuesday, September 16, 1862 [translation]

La Minerve of Montreal expressed often the views of George Cartier, and Cartier was already a supporter of the Intercolonial Railway.

" . . . The government paper in question [Montreal *L'Ordre*] has always been openly hostile to the intercolonial railway. That railway [so it says] will lead to frightful misfortunes for French Canadians; in the future it will probably bring about confederation of the Provinces, followed by anglicisation and religious persecution.

"We condemn this exaggerated fear and remind our fellow newspaper that its own leaders were themselves once in favour of this great enterprise. . . .

"For our part we wish this colonial enterprise every success, whether carried out by our political friends or our opponents."

71 THE NEED FOR A DECISIVE POLICY

Leader, Toronto
Tuesday, October 14, 1862

The editorial below, from the leading Conservative paper in Toronto, is full of the cold, good sense of a paper (and a party) in opposition to the Government. It was also quoted, November 1, 1862, by the Halifax *Acadian Recorder*.

"No great achievement is easy of accomplishment; and the glory of success is in proportion to difficulties overcome. Unless united, British America cannot hope to prepare herself for those duties of nationality which may be forced upon her before she is in a position to exercise them. There is no use in disguising the fact; scarcely any interest is felt in the question of Colonial Union. The habit of living from hand to mouth, which politicians have contracted — of dealing only with the question of the hour and leaving the future to take care of itself — has become so inveterate, that it is generally felt to be a bore to take a wider and more comprehensive view of our actual position and of that future which, not distant, is to decide the destiny of these Provinces, and determine the part they are hereafter to play on this continent. . . .

"The Intercolonial railway is the first step; and it is a most important one."

72 THE INTERCOLONIAL RAILWAY AND NATIONALISM

Leader, Toronto
Saturday, October 25, 1862

"A great country such as Nature has destined this to be would not be justified in refusing to acquire a winter sea-port, when the object can be obtained upon reasonable terms. Without it, what is the possible future of Canada? A back country, with no access to the seaboard, during six months of the year, but through the territory of a foreign power, occupies a position of deplorable dependence. It holds its existence on suffrance; and it must certainly feel that the indulgence is at any time liable to be withdrawn. We ought to have pride enough to desire to be independent of any foreign country in all the essentials of national life. This is every day becoming more and more the general feeling of the country."

73 QUESTIONING THE ADVANTAGES OF THE PROPOSED INTERCOLONIAL RAILWAY

Weekly Dispatch, St. Thomas
Thursday, November 13, 1862

"What possible benefit can Canada derive from developing the resources of Nova Scotia, New Brunswick or the North West Territory. If the Intercolonial Railway was going to cut through rich portions of the fertile lands of Canada, like the Grand Trunk . . . there might be some reason to talk [as McGee does] of further development; but when it can only push our produce some five or six hundred miles further by rail through a barren country, when we can now send it by sea or by Portland, and thereby make a commercial mart of

Halifax instead of Montreal or Quebec, such development becomes mere delusion."

74 THE CONSERVATIVES' ATTITUDE TOWARD THE INTERCOLONIAL RAILWAY

Morning Chronicle, Quebec
Monday, January 19, 1863

That the Reform party were unhappy with the Intercolonial Railway is understood, but it is clear, from this editorial in the Conservative standard-bearer in Quebec City, at this time the capital, that Conservatives were not exactly enthusiastic.

"The Intercolonial Railway, then, has to be shelved. The deputation to England were not successful in their negotiation with the Imperial Government. Under all the circumstances of the Province this is a failure that will cause but little regret. Not that the undertaking was undesirable; not that, in a strategic [*sic*] point of view, it would not afford facilities that are doubtless wanting; but because the economic interests of the country are not essentially involved in its consummation, and because the moment is not favorable for the further augmentation of pecuniary liability. The question of a railway to a British port on the Atlantic is simply a question of time for Canada, and has doubtless to be built — the questions are when and how."

75 CRITICISM OF THE GOVERNMENT'S SHIFTING POLICY TOWARD THE INTERCOLONIAL RAILWAY

Leader, Toronto
Friday, October 2, 1863

"The [1862 Intercolonial Railway] agreement was definite. . . . Upon what facts our Government came to such an agreement as this we have never been told; but now they venture the interesting information that then they were groping entirely in the dark; they knew nothing about the route the proposed road was to take; nothing about the amount it would cost — in fact, nothing at all. . . . Through the smallest possible hole they creep out of an engagement, solemnly entered into with the Lower Provinces. By a confession of their own ignorance and incompetency they effectually burk [*sic*] the Intercolonial railway scheme, at the same time endeavoring to make a show of consistency. It is such conduct as this that has tended to bring our Government into disrepute and destroyed our credit in England. If the Ministry are opposed to the Intercolonial railway it would be honorable in them to say so openly and plainly. But with their present shuffling, indecisive course, any honorable man must feel disgusted."

76 A LOWER CANADA VIEW OF NOVA SCOTIAN ATTITUDES

Quebec Daily News, Quebec
Saturday, November 17, 1863

A Quebec paper comments on Nova Scotian interest in schemes of political change. This editorial was copied and reprinted in the Halifax *Morning Chronicle*, December 3, 1863.

"For probably forty years the most prominent politicians and public men of Nova Scotia have been clamoring for some Colonial system which would give a larger scope to their intellectual activity, than they imagine they can find in their native Province. Colonial representation in the Imperial Parliament was the panacea of Mr. Howe; that the patronage of the Empire should be so disposed of as to give Colonists places and advantages for nothing [,] which native Englishmen have to pay for, was the modest and feasible proposition of Mr. [T.C.] Haliburton. A union of all British America, which it seemed to be would in that event be intellectually represented by Nova Scotia (on the success of Sam Slick), was the next favorite conception of the leading Nova Scotians."

77 SINCERITY OF THE GOVERNMENT TOWARD THE INTERCOLONIAL RAILWAY PROJECT QUESTIONED

Quebec Daily News, Quebec
Saturday, December 5, 1863

"We fear those homeopathic doses of reproof, administered to the people of New Brunswick by the Quebec organ [the *Quebec Daily Mercury,* organ of the Sandfield Macdonald government], will not remove the irritation they feel, and very energetically express. . . . The mission [of Sicotte and Howland to London] was abortive because the British Minister insisted on the creation of a sinking fund [for the Intercolonial railway loan], as a sort of collateral security from the Provinces. We believe the Lower Provinces were prepared to accept this condition of the arrangement. That at least serves us as a proof of their sincerity. But our ambassadors, feigned surprise. . . . In fact our deputies miffed, or pretended to miff at the unreasonable condition of a sinking fund. . . . the objection raised by Messrs. Sicotte and Howland to a sinking fund was more than puerile; we fear it was worse. . . . we believe now . . . that our Government never was sincere about the Intercolonial Railway project. . . .

"But to save appearances the public were to be cajoled with a survey, and the Government let softly down . . . in the present critically balanced state of parties, the Premier could not afford to coquette with a single vote. . . . the scheme in the hands of the present administration has been sacrificed to party policy, and party necessity. Our fellow subjects in the Lower Provinces may depend on it, that while Mr. Dorion is in the cabinet, there will be no Inter-Colonial Railway."

78 FEDERATION: THE DESTINY OF CANADA

Globe, Toronto
Wednesday, November 25, 1863

On November 5, 1863, the Halifax *Morning Chronicle* had said, in the stress of the fiasco over the Intercolonial Railway, that "the Maritime Provinces will never consent to any union or political connection of any kind with the upper country." The following is a reply.

"The union of all British America is not a question of gain with us; it is one of political *prestige* and nationality. It is favourably viewed by our population. We look forward to it as our destiny. But it is not a scheme which we feel ourselves compelled to undertake at once by any pressing necessity. No interest suffers by our refraining from action. We are only postponing an indefinite — and by many considered a doubtful — good to a more convenient season, when existing obstacles will, it is hoped, be removed from our path."

C. The Northwest, 1859-1863

Red River's main characteristic was uncertainty about its future. The Hudson's Bay Company inquiry in London in 1857 and Canadian interest in the Northwest had wrought some changes. Troops of the Royal Canadian Rifles, a British regiment stationed in Canada, were sent out in 1857. They were withdrawn, rather to the chagrin of the people of Red River, in August, 1861, leaving as they had come, via York Factory. Two months later the Americans announced the creation of Dakota Territory. The juxtaposition of American energy and British supineness was a fertile source of envy and unease in Red River.

The Canadian expeditions westward of 1857, 1858, and the great Dawson-Hind Report of 1859 to the Canadian legislature signalled a sharp rise in Canadian interest in Red River. But none of this produced much concrete change. Canada's Conservative government was unwilling to purchase Rupert's Land, believing, quite rightly, that for a generation to come it would be quite expensive enough just to administer the country. What a great many people of Red River wanted, and would continue to prefer, was being made a Crown Colony, as Vancouver Island had been in 1858, and thus put under the direct administration of the Colonial Office. This the British Government were most unwilling to do. The irritation in Red River at this apparent dead end of their political future is manifest.

As yet the two Pacific colonies, Vancouver Island and British Columbia, were too far away to be swung much within the orbit of political union. There was considerable interest in the east in the Fraser River gold rush that started in 1858 and was to last until 1863. It was the ending of the gold rush, and its consequent repercussions on the economy of the two colonies that was to start them thinking about Confederation.

79 POSITION OF RED RIVER IN COLONIAL FEDERATION

Nor'Wester, Red River
Friday, February 1, 1861

The first issues of the Red River *Nor'Wester* appeared on December 28, 1859, published by two Canadians, William Buckingham and William Coldwell. It is sometimes said the paper reflected Canadian interests; but while it may have done so later on, in 1869 under Dr. Schultz, at this period at least, it echoed Red River sentiments.

"The next session of the Canadian Parliament will take up the Extended Confederation scheme, without a doubt, and the policy that will tend most to strengthen the influence of British America is the creation of a federal head, allowing Newfoundland, Nova Scotia, New Brunswick, (including Prince Edward's Island), Canada East, Canada West, the Red River country as a colony, and British Columbia, seven in all, to take their places as independent and sovereign states, making their own local laws, and having control of their own affairs; each half of Canada assuming their fair quota of the public debt, and each member of the Confederation receiving a fixed portion of the general revenue. . . . "

80 AMERICAN PROCLIVITIES IN RED RIVER

Nor'Wester, Red River
Wednesday, February 5, 1862

This editorial produced marked sympathy in Canada. Even the Quebec *Morning Chronicle*, the Conservative standard-bearer, thought the British Government should do something, and the theme was taken up still more powerfully in the Toronto *Globe*, May 14, 1862.

"The very peculiar system of government which prevails in this country bids fair to drive us into annexation to the United States. Popular opinion runs strongly in this direction. . . . Americanism has become rampant with all classes, ages and conditions. Even old Scotchmen and Englishmen — men born and brought up in the old country, and heretofore strongly British in their feelings and preferences — now join in the general outcry against the British connection, and charge their change of sentiment to our utterly un-British form of government, and to the indifference of the Home Government. What is the use — say they — of being connected with Britain when the connection is merely nominal? It is a mere name, an empty sound. . . . in the Red River country, the British connection is worthless."

81 NEED TO SETTLE THE CLAIMS OF THE HUDSON'S BAY COMPANY

Nor'Wester, Red River
Wednesday, May 28, 1862

"Can it be expected that we should not become Americanized, when on the one hand Britain shows perfect indifference to us, and we enjoy none of the commercial or governmental advantages which we have a right to expect — and on the other hand, American influences of every kind are operating upon us? . . . Almost any week from May to October inclusive, a splendid steamboat may be seen at Fort Garry discharging her cargo of goods, and taking off packages of furs for the St. Paul, Boston, or New York market: whose boat is this? American citizens, whose enterprise, in the eyes of Red Riverites, throws into the shade the slow-going do-nothing Britons, whom nevertheless, we are expected to admire, imitate. . . . the people of Red River now say to England — Do something for us at once, or forever give us up and let us shape our own destinies. . . . Now, moreover, is a fit time to settle once for all the question of the Hudson's Bay Company. We do not agree with those who clamor for an abrupt, unceremonious and unconditional termination of the Company's *status* in this country, for this would be doing a gross injustice to very many innocent persons. . . . A peaceful and equitable settlement of the Company's claim is, therefore, an urgent *desideratum.*"

Section II

British North America 1864-1867

A. Colonists and Conferences, April - December, 1864

The eight months in 1864 witnessed a real metamorphosis in the affairs of British North America. The movement for Maritime union had started in Nova Scotia and New Brunswick in February and March; that was followed, almost at once, by a constitutional crisis in the Canadas in April, and another one in June. These two crises provided the precedents and the justification for the formation of a coalition government in the Province of Canada. It was this coalition of Conservatives and Reformers that was to bring about Confederation.

The Confederation movement in the Province of Canada and the Maritime union movement in Nova Scotia and New Brunswick came together at Charlottetown, Prince Edward Island, on September 1, 1864. Maritime union was abandoned — Prince Edward Island was not interested in it anyway — and the other delegates warmly supported the idea of Confederation. Details were hammered out, not without difficulty, at Quebec in October.

By that time, the St. Alban's Raid had pointed up a weighty problem in the Province of Canada's relations with the United States, and one that was exacerbated in December with the release of the Confederate "raiders" by a Canadian court in Montreal. By this time, too, the British Government had enthusiastically endorsed the Quebec Resolutions, and the debate upon them was launched in the British North American newspapers.

There had been much speculation and comment already on Confederation and the form it should take, even before the Charlottetown Conference. But now, in December, there was to be something definite to go on, and the real promise of implementation almost at once if colonial legislatures approved.

Movement for Coalition in the Province of Canada

The movement for coalition grew perceptibly in the early months of 1864. There had been some tentative but ineffectual discussions between Macdonald and Brown — though through an intermediary — in 1862 and again in 1863. Meanwhile the Sandfield Macdonald government staggered on, in imminent danger of defeat since September, 1863. In March, 1864, Sandfield Macdonald approached Sir Etienne Taché, the French Conservative leader. Lord Monck, the Governor-General, believed a coalition government would be much the best thing for the Province. Sandfield Macdonald's attempt failed, however, perhaps because the important question of the purpose and basis of such a coalition was not really answered. His government collapsed on March 21, 1864.

It was replaced by a Conservative administration led by Sir Etienne Taché and John A. Macdonald. Shortly after the formation of that government, George Brown secured approval in the Assembly for a select committee to report upon federation as a solution for Canada's difficulties. It carried on May 19, 1864, despite the opposition of the Government. Brown's committee reported on June 14, 1864. To no one's surprise, their answer was federation of the Canadas. That same day, the Conservative government was defeated on another issue by two votes.

It was then that George Brown and John A. Macdonald finally met to discuss coalition. The basis of it was Confederation. If Confederation could not be achieved, the Canadians would set up a federation of the two Canadas by themselves.

1 DISCONTENT WITH THE PRESENT UNION

Aurora Banner, Aurora
Friday, April 1, 1864

"The frequent changes in Canadian administrations demonstrate that a defect is in the public system. . . . Here are two Provinces of different nationalities — of different languages — of different religions — and to a great extent of different customs: these two Provinces are professedly united, while in reality they are at variance, and to all appearances there is no prospect of their ever acting in unison."

2 PLEA FOR STRONGER LEADERSHIP

Quebec Daily News, Quebec
Thursday, June 16, 1864

The Taché-Macdonald government fell on June 14, 1864, and the gloom that event occasioned is palpable.

"The politics of the country are again in a state of chaos. Another Ministerial crisis — the fourth within two years — has taken place, and judging from the disposition and temper of the two parties into which the Legislature is so equally divided, there will likely be no end of them . . . . What the result of the present Ministerial crisis may be, we cannot say. It may end in dissolution, or in a coalition of the more moderate elements on each side of the House . . . . Every one feels that a strong Government is wanted; that an infusion of a new element in the Councils of the Province is desirable. Let us have it as speedily as possible. . . . "

3 BROWN AND THE CHARGE OF INCONSISTENCY

Globe, Toronto
Saturday, June 18, 1864

On the afternoon of Friday, June 17, 1864, Macdonald announced in the Assembly that a coalition with George Brown was being proposed with the purpose of settling the constitutional difficulties of the Province of Canada. The following editorial in the *Globe* was written about twelve hours afterwards.

"We cannot doubt that Mr. Brown, in responding to the appeal of his old political opponents' [sic] felt, in all its gravity, the danger of misconception which he ran. He could not forget the past. He could not forget how often, and how strongly, he has denounced Ministerial coalitions as utterly demoralizing. . . . But assuredly, if the immense importance of the object to be attained could justify such a step, Mr. Brown amply has it for the position he now occupies. . . . "

4 ON GEORGE BROWN'S HIGH-MINDEDNESS

Quebec Daily News, Quebec
Monday, June 20, 1864

"He is too shrewd not to have perceived that the duties of a legislator rise far above the gratification of personal malice, and that even the interests of party must give way to public exigency. Besides he observed the more prominent leaders of the opposition recklessly making shipwreck of their reputation, sinking the dignity of the statesman into the gratification of personal revenge, he saw that the men who affected to ignore his position as leader, and who tried to degrade him into a mere party hack, were fast becoming bankrupt. . . . Now, Mr. Brown is not like too many of his colleagues, a mere trickster in politics; his views are too large to be for ever grubbing up personal detraction, and substituting that for policy."

5 THE REFORM PARTY AND FEDERAL UNION

Globe, Toronto
Wednesday, June 22, 1864

The parliamentary caucus of the Reform party met at the Kent House, Quebec City on the morning of Tuesday, June 21, 1864, to approve the question of a coalition with the Conservative party on the Confederation issue. It was carried 34 to 5. Among the five was John Sandfield Macdonald, MPP Cornwall.

Reform caucus resolution: "That we approve of the course which has been pursued by Mr. Brown in the negotiations with the Government, and that we approve of the project of a Federal Union of the Canadas, with provision for its extension to the Maritime Provinces and the North-Western Territory, as one basis on which the constitutional difficulties now existing could be settled."

6 BROWN'S SPEECH TO PARLIAMENT

Globe, Toronto
Thursday, June 23, 1864

Report of Brown's Speech of June 22, 1864.

"Nothing but a most stern sense of duty could have brought me into such a position. I have struggled to avoid entering the Cabinet . . . [but now] let us try to rise superior to the pitifulness of party politics in the interests of our country; let us unite to consider and settle this question as a great national issue, in a manner worthy of us as a people. (Enthusiastic cheers.) . . . And one thing I must say. It is little sacrifice to me to accept this compromise. It is comparatively little even for the member for Sherbrooke (Mr. Galt) to accept this compromise. But it was a great thing, a most bold and manly thing, for Sir Etienne Taché, and for the member for Montreal East (Mr. Cartier) to take up this question. . . . I do frankly confess, Mr. Speaker, that if I never had any other parliamentary successes than that which I achieved this day . . . I would have desired no greater honour for my children to keep years hence in their remembrance, than that I had a hand however humble, in the accomplishment of that work.'

"The hon. gentleman resumed his seat amidst loud and prolonged cheering from all parts of the House, and when the sitting was immediately afterwards suspended for dinner recess, many members of both sections of the Province and from both sides of the House, crowded around him to offer their congratulations."

7 THE SURPRISE AND SUDDENNESS OF CONFEDERATION, EVEN IN CANADA

Quebec Daily News, Quebec
Friday, June 24, 1864

"The scheme for the pacification of both sections of the Province . . . caused intense surprise, as much by the suddenness of its revelations as by the comprehensive measures it disclosed . . . . Hardly a single speaker [in the Assembly debate] objected to the scheme on the ground that it was not needed. All conceded that it was indispensable; that in the critical relation of affairs between Upper and Lower Canada, this measure of federation had become an absolute necessity; that we had reached a point beyond which we could not proceed without imminent danger. . . . "

8 PRESENT NEED FOR MEN OF PRINCIPLE IN GOVERNMENT

Hastings Chronicle, Belleville
Wednesday, July 20, 1864

"Mr. Brown, unlike those who have preceded him from his side of the House, has only gone into a Government when he could take his principles with him. . . . Mr. Brown carries the constitutional question by the very act of joining the Government. . . . It was by the formation of the three several previous Cabinets and their three several failures, which educated public opinion. . . . Nothing but a strong conviction of the necessity and patriotism of the conduct of the gentlemen who have thrown off party trammels for the good of the country, could have averted the hostile criticism which even the best men under like circumstances would have a right to expect."

9 CANADA LETTER, JULY 13, 1864

Weekly British Colonist, Victoria
Tuesday, August 23, 1864

"During a thirty year's residence in Canada I have never seen a period like the present. The political Pandora's box has been literally shut, and all the animosities and heart burnings appear to be enclosed. . . . Never was a man more bepraised than George Brown. All classes vie with each other in lauding him for his patriotism and self-abnegation. In fact no other man in Canada durst have ventured on the same ground. If he succeeds, as I trust he will, he will be the greatest man in this Canada of ours. If he fails he loses all his popularity and influence, and doubtless many will blame him for his temerity in trusting his hereditary foes. . . . Never in my recollection has the Fourth Estate been so unanimous on any question."

Approaches to the Charlottetown Conference and the Canadian visit to the Maritimes of August, 1864

Maritime union was never a very active issue in either New Brunswick or Nova Scotia, but it had generated enough force in the spring of 1864 for both colonial legislatures to pass resolutions authorizing the appointment of delegates to a Maritime union conference. Prince Edward Island passed resolutions authorizing delegates to discuss, not Maritime union, but the expediency of it. There is an important difference. Prince Edward Island had no use for any union that would deprive the Island of its legislature, but it was felt that it was courteous to give the whole question an airing.

But no date or place for such a conference had been set when, on June 30, 1864, the Canadians officially asked to be allowed to come. Then there was action. The Maritime union conference was called to meet at Charlottetown on Thursday, September 1, 1864.

The Canadian visit to Nova Scotia and New Brunswick in August, 1864 came quite independently and, in fact, fortuitously. It arose from a conversation in the winter of 1863-64 between Sandford Fleming and D'Arcy McGee. McGee had been in Halifax in July, 1863, and had been struck by the fact that Canadians and Maritimers hardly knew one another. "What does a Canadian look like?" It was a perfectly possible question. McGee himself was one of the few Canadians that had ever been in Halifax. The upshot was that the Saint John and Halifax Chambers of Commerce agreed to sponsor a visit. Invitations went out in May and June, 1864, to Canadian newspapermen and to a substantial number of MPP's.

With Confederation now in the air, the Canadians availed themselves of the opportunity with a will. Nearly one hundred came. The whole adventure was blessed with sublime weather, plenty of Maritime hospitality (both solid and liquid varieties), and a plethora of enthusiastic speeches about Union. It was in fact just what the Confederation movement at that point most needed.

10 ON THE MARITIME UNION DEBATE IN THE LEGISLATURE

Halifax Citizen, Halifax
Tuesday, March 29, 1864

"Every sincere advocate of Colonial Union [*i.e.,* Maritime union] must regret the dulness [*sic*] of this debate. The indifference exhibited was most chilling. . . . A valuable impulse can scarcely be expected from vapid generalities, listlessly uttered and indolently heard."

11 PRINCE EDWARD ISLAND AND UNION

Islander, Charlottetown
Friday, June 24, 1864

" . . . [Maritime union] at the present time, appears to be attracting but little attention among our neighbors. Their Press scarcely ever alludes to it.

In this Island, however, the newspapers have generally declared against it, and it is seldom that one meets, among the agriculturalists, a man who will listen to anything in favor of a proposition which would deprive the Colony of its existence as a separate Government . . . .

"[As for the Province of Canada government, it] has already become *all but* an impossibility; and we should think that the statesmen of that great Province must see that they cannot much longer continue as they are — that they must seek in a *repeal* of the Union of Upper and Lower or in a further *Union*, the remedy for these causes which now prevent the formation of a Government possessing any elements of stability."

---

12 FEDERATION: A PANACEA OR AN IDEAL?

Daily Evening Globe, Saint John
Monday, June 30, 1864

"The people of the Lower Provinces can feel very little confidence in the sudden federative scheme proposed in Canada. . . . The sooner we are united the better; but it is not very satisfying nor gratifying to us to find that a scheme with this end in view is suddenly proposed in Canada, not for the general good, or with any grand object in view, but simply to settle some Canadian local differences. . . . We believe our people would willingly unite with Canada to make a great country of these Provinces. . . . But they would have much more confidence in the scheme if it had been propounded on its own merits and not to save the Canadian Parliament from dissolution."

13 A REVIEW OF THE SITUATION WITH REGARD TO FEDERATION

Head Quarters, Fredericton
Wednesday, July 6, 1864

An early, and remarkably prophetic editorial on the forthcoming Maritime Union conference at Charlottetown.

"Everybody here will cordially wish the Canadians, Upper and Lower, a happy issue out of all their troubles . . . . A strong effort will be made [by the Canadians] to include all the Provinces in the scheme of Federation, but it is not in human nature . . . to be expected that the people of the Lower Provinces, seeing their neighbors in tribulation and trouble, will cheerfully and willingly hazard their own peace by joining their fortunes, for better or worse, to a country in which the elements of dissension are strong, and which is larger and richer than themselves. They may wish for union, but they may like to see the experiment of Federation tried on the lesser scale (as applied to the Canadas alone) before they will agree to enter in it at the door that has been so kindly left open for them. But no doubt the effort will be made. It is reported that Mr. D'Arcy M'Gee and a number of leading political men in Canada, will visit Halifax and St. John in the course of the summer. Of course they will be well and hospitably entertained, but very possibly . . . the Canadians may yet be deceived as to the amount of cordiality that a proposition for a Federation of all the Provinces will at this time be received.

" . . . They [New Brunswickers] now know that the conference of delegates from the Lower Provinces, on the subject of [Maritime] Union, is to be a matter of fact, and that it is going to take place in Charlottetown in the course of the summer. Delegates from Canada are to be present in order to open up the question of a Federal

Union of all the Provinces. The people here will naturally be anxious, or at least curious, to know what the result of that conference will be, and the effect of the presence of the Canadian delegates at it. Possibly the entrance of the Canadian delegates into the Conference at Charlottetown will have no other effect than of giving the Lower Province delegates an opportunity to evade the question of a Union of the Maritime Provinces, to put it off . . . until it is seen how the Federative principle will work as applied to Canada alone. But, possibly, on the other hand, the delegates may entertain the proposition of the Canadians seriously, and may see in the Federal principle an escape from the difficulties that lie in the way of an Union of the Lower Provinces, and conclude to recommend in their report a Federation of all the Provinces."

---

14 SUPPORT FOR THE UNION OF BRITISH AMERICA

Acadian Recorder, Halifax
Saturday, July 30, 1864

The editorial below represents the position of the *Acadian Recorder* right through to 1867.

"A certain portion of the press in Canada is vigilantly advocating just now what is called the doctrine of Federation. It is said first that Canadians must abandon legislative union and substitute Federal union. We have carefully read the arguments put forth to this end and we cannot admit their sufficiency. . . . The federal principle, let us remember, is at the root of the American war. If it had not been claimed as an element of the Federal constitution that each state had a sovereign right, irrespective of the central government, we never should have heard of secession. . . . If we should unite these British provinces

into a Federation, what guarantee have we that some of them shall not some day play the game of Virginia, Carolina & Co. Is not the right of secession — a kind of petty state sovereignty — somehow knotted up with the Federal principle? Some day, no doubt, a grand national structure will rise here in northern North America, but if the Federal principle is introduced, it may lurk like a Guy Fawkes under the building. . . . Let us take warning by the half-way work of Canada. . . . If Canada is to come to our [Maritime union] conference we beg that she may not come with her mouth full of 'Federal' preaching, that she may come with a determination to pave the way to cement British America into one indivisible whole. We must have our Maritime Union first. The larger union will come in its proper time."

---

15 CAUTION URGED CONCERNING THE QUESTION OF UNION

Daily Evening Globe, Saint John
Thursday, August 4, 1864

The above editorial of the Halifax *Acadian Recorder*, July 30, 1864 is quoted and supported in part by the Saint John paper.

"We cordially agree with our Halifax contemporary . . . that we should not be in a hurry. The proposed federation has burst upon us so suddenly that we have not yet had time calmly to look at it. Our people have given it no consideration, although we have all at different times had our dreams of a future when the British possessions in America should become one great nation. For the first time we are being brought face to face with the reality. . . . "

---

16 POLITICAL EXPEDIENCY REJECTED IN FEDERATION

Morning Chronicle, Halifax
Thursday, August 4, 1864

If there is going to be a conference on Confederation, it "ought certainly soon to be organized. . . .

"A proposition for a Federal Union, however — any scheme that is to utilize the Maritime Provinces as make weights for balancing the machinery of new, untried, and more than doubtful expediency adapted to the exigencies of Canadian necessities — is not likely, we fear, to find favor in any of the Lower Provinces."

---

17 THE LARGER ISSUES INVOLVED IN UNION

Quebec Daily News, Quebec
Tuesday, August 16, 1864

"The popular sentiment [about Confederation] is, that it was adopted as the only available mode to disentangle the difficulties of Government and remove an impediment to legislation; and this opinion to a certain extent is quite correct. But now as the subject is more generally discussed, more critically examined, its proportions become enlarged; and we discover that it embraces issues of a magnitude greater than most people at first imagined." These issues are mainly, the whole question of defence, and of relations with Great Britain.

---

18 A NEW BRUNSWICK VIEW OF INTERNAL CANADIAN POLITICS

Morning Telegraph, Saint John
Saturday, August 13, 1864

"It must be borne in mind, that there are many opponents of any Union 'now and forever', some conscientiously of the opinion that matters and things are better as they are; others will oppose for the mere sake of opposition, while a third party will strenuously advocate a Union of the Lower Provinces, leaving Canada out in the cold. . . .

"It will be well if the hon. gentlemen [George Brown] does not mistake the wishes of these Lower Colonies also. While the [Toronto] *Globe* 'belittles' the latter in its editorials, and plumes the Canadas as a mighty nation without them, he will do well to remember that large numbers of Lower Provincialists are by no means enamoured with the past history of Canada — its manifest corruption; its bitter intestine broils; its diversities of Nationalities and Religions which have become intensely political. . . . It would be well, therefore, if these Lower Provinces cultivated a more honorable appreciation, just at its proper value, of their big sister, and while willing to acknowledge her many charms, remember that she has not monopolized all loveliness. . . . We disdain to be considered her menial or to seek a postilion's position in any family arrangement in which we should be equal."

---

19 ARRIVAL OF THE CANADIAN PARTY

Daily Evening Globe, Saint John
Thursday, August 18, 1864

On the Canadian visit of August, 1864, a report by the *Globe's* Halifax correspondent.

"Our [Canadian] visitors have met with a reception which far eclipses anything ever heard of in the annals of the Province [of Nova Scotia]. . . . A most fortunate thing for us has been the fineness of the weather. The days have been cloudless and at night the moon has shown in all her glory . . . . There have been no politics at all this last week. The greatest political enemies have been for a time the greatest friends. . . . "

20 A CANADIAN REPORT ON MARITIME ATTITUDES

Leader, Toronto
Saturday, August 20, 1864.

Report of their correspondent from Halifax, Tuesday, August 16, 1864.

"I think I may say with the fullest confidence that there is no earnest desire among the people of Nova Scotia or New Brunswick to change their state at present. . . . let us not unnecessarily hasten on the day when this result shall be achieved. . . . Strain events out of their natural order and confusion and not union will be the result.

"There has not been in these Provinces a tithe of the political agitation which has distracted Canada; and the consequence is a large share of general satisfaction. The people here are rather content to suffer the ills they bear than fly to others that they know not of. . . . It is argued by such men as Mr. Howe that Federal union will not accomplish this object [union of British North America.] It [federal union] will not make us a great people. It will not elevate our thoughts or enlarge our minds; but rather sow the seed of future division. . . .

" [As for legislative union], it would be something to be a citizen of a great Northern Kingdom, one in feeling, one in the spirit of self-defence, one in everything which marks a great and free people. It may be said that this is Utopian. I give no opinion. I simply state what is the feeling here, and that feeling must be consulted."

21 HALIFAX AND SAINT JOHN DESCRIBED AND COMPARED

Leader, Toronto
Monday, August 22, 1864

Report of its correspondent from Saint John, August 17, 1864.

"Halifax . . . is much more aristocratic than Saint John. There is a courtly air about it. It takes pride in its magnificent club house; its bloods drive fast horses and ride in dog carts*; its dry goods clerks ape the manners, and talk the talk of Cockney swells; its ladies dress in the height of fashion, read the latest novels as well in the language of Madame George Sand and Eugene de Balzac** as in their native tongue. . . . It is far different with the commercial of New Brunswick. *There* no courtly influence is felt. Its people are more matter of fact; go about their business as if their business were all of life to them . . . appear generally like people more disposed to make money and put it away for the future use. . . . "

*A dog cart is a fast two-wheeled driving cart.
**Should be Honoré de Balzac.

22 FEDERATION, INDEPENDENCE AND LOCAL AUTONOMY

Examiner, Charlottetown
Monday, August 22, 1864

Union Question, No. 1

"Scarcely any of the Colonial Delegates who will meet here in September will differ materially from Mr. [George] Coles as to the importance and necessity of maintaining our separate local governments as they now exist, or nearly so. Men in office will not be inclined to sacrifice their local status by voting for the abolition of their local Legislature — men *out* of office will not be disposed to do so either, because they hope one day to be *in*. But the great people abroad everywhere, whose souls are untainted by the lust of petty power, are still more strongly opposed than the petty politicians to the abrogation of our local Legislatures. They think, and especially those in remote sections, perhaps justly enough, that under one large Parliament, legislating hundreds of miles away their wants would not be as well cared for as they would be by a Parliament sitting within a day's drive of all of them, and directly under the control of all. When a man pays taxes he does it grudgingly, but it is nevertheless a consolation to his troubled spirit to see the money laid out in improvements all around him . . . .

"Shall we, then, think seriously about a Federal Union. We believe we ought. Great Britain is constantly urging upon our attention a Union of some kind. The only kind of Union we can have is a Federal one. That means little or nothing short of separation from Great Britain. . . . If we make up our minds for an Independent Federation . . . we must prepare to bid goodbye to old Mother England, and to lay on the shelf with other rubbish those antiquated notions of loyalty for which she herself has not now that sentimental regard with which they were cherished in the days of 'auld lang syne.' "

23 DIFFERENT ATTITUDES OF THE CANADAS AND THE MARITIMES TOWARD UNION

Quebec Daily News, Quebec
Thursday, August 25, 1864

Juxtaposition of the necessities of Canada and of the Maritime colonies.

"No men in this country have ever

undertaken the discharge of graver or more solemn responsibility. That they feel the weight and importance of their duty is plain. . . . The question of federation with the maritime Po - vinrces [*sic*], is not with them as with us, one of urgency. Their Governments are not pledged to it; the rancour of party has not pushed them to the brink of a bitter sectional conflict, from which there is no escape, except through this expedient. Nor, from what we learn are their people so devotedly anxious for federation, as to accept it without a long and careful examination. That the idea of federation is favorably entertained, there is no doubt; but that it has penetrated little below the surface of society, except with a few reflecting men, is pretty clear."

24 FEDERAL UNION NOT ON THE AGENDA

Daily Evening Globe, Saint John
Monday, August 29, 1864

Nova Scotia and New Brunswick should be able to agree on Maritime Union, with or without Prince Edward Island. Canada, however, comes to Charlottetown uninvited, and any discussions of British North American federal union will be informal.

"The delegates from the Lower Provinces must all feel the embarrasing position in which they are placed by Canada: but they must also feel that if they adopt, as the basis of their deliberations, a scheme different from that which they were appointed to consider, they will not be carrying out the legitimate objects of their mission. . . . "

The Charlottetown Conference

The Charlottetown Conference met in Charlottetown, Prince Edward Island from Thursday, September 1, to Wednesday, September 7. It agreed to postpone consideration of Maritime union in order to hear the Canadians with their proposals of Confederation. It met again in Halifax, September 10-12, again in Saint John on September 14. By that time it was agreed the Quebec Conference would meet on October 10. The Charlottetown Conference did, however, meet again to discuss Maritime union, at Toronto on November 3. It was agreed to postpone consideration of Maritime union in view of the negotiations for Confederation. The Conference was then adjourned *sine die*.

25 CHARLOTTETOWN DESCRIBED

Morning Telegraph, Saint John
Wednesday, August 31, 1864

A description of Charlottetown, by the *Telegraph's* special Charlottetown correspondent.

"The ochreous soil of the banks [of Charlottetown harbour] forms a pretty setting for the opal waters of the bay, and gives an enviable prominence to the green fields of grain that are spread out luxuriantly above them. There are neat white cottages scattered along the shores, and some pretentious residences near the city surrounded by sheltering groves of fir, and overlooking the bay. The city itself lies on a slight elevation; the houses are chiefly of a Quakerish drab and brown hue, clustered together methodically; there is very little foliage in the densest part, the straight parallel streets run down to the water's edge like the red lines of a ledger. . . . There is nothing attractive above the business part of Charlottetown. . . . The streets are clean, except when the wind blows and raises a dust, which flies upon the smallest provocation."

26 THE QUESTION OF FEDERATION AND ITS PLACE IN THE CHARLOTTETOWN CONFERENCE

Monitor, Charlottetown
Thursday, September 1, 1864

Both branches of the Prince Edward Island legislature have pronounced against Maritime union. Prince Edward Island delegates were appointed to the Maritime union conference, "we presume, because it was felt that it would not be treating our neighbors with due courtesy to refuse even to listen to what they might have to say on the subject. As far, however, as the Island is concerned, we have no hesitation in saying that all attempts to bring about a '*legislative* union' of the Provinces will be stoutly resisted both by the people and legislature of this Island. If, therefore, the Conference which is to assemble here to-day is to be productive of any very beneficial results, 'a wider range' will have to be given to its deliberations than appears to have been originally intended. This, we are inclined to think, will inevitably be the case, since Canada also will be represented at the Conference, and her proposition is, not a 'legislative' but a 'federal' union of all the Provinces, — a scheme which, we are free to admit, is viewed with much greater favor by our people than any other yet propounded. We agree, therefore, with the [Saint John, N. B. *Morning*] *News* that the delegates from the Lower Provinces should 'give any propositions that the Canadian representatives may offer a careful hearing,' and that 'it is their bounden duty to discuss the question of federation, so far as affects the North American Provinces irrespective of limit. . . . ' "

27 CRITICISM OVER THE RECEPTION OF THE DELEGATES

Vindicator, Charlottetown
Wednesday, September 7, 1864

"Much indignation has been excited in the community generally against the Government at the manner in which the delegates from Canada, New Brunswick, and Nova Scotia have been received. When the Nova Scotians arrived, there was no one on the wharf to receive them, and they were allowed to find, as best they could, their way to a hotel. The Canadians arrived on Thursday [September 1st] . . . and after the steamer had been at anchor for some time, the Colonial Secretary — the only official we believe, in attendance — started in a canoe or flat-bottomed boat, with a barrel of flour in the bow, and two jars of molasses in the stern, and with a lusty fisherman as his only companion. . . . We can better imagine the feelings of the Canadians than describe them as they witnessed the exertions of Mr. Secretary Pope to reach the *Victoria,* and still more so when they learned his official character. . . . The Canadians were under the necessity — as were the Nova Scotians — of hunting up quarters for themselves, some of whom found their way into Eckstadt's Oyster Saloon. . . . "

28 THE PROS AND CONS OF FEDERATION

Protestant, Charlottetown
Saturday, September 10, 1864

" . . . they [the Canadians] have decoyed them [the Maritime delegates] clean away from legislative Union — the small egg which they met to hatch — by holding out to their view the ostrich egg of Confederation, which of course they will have to leave in the sand of uncertainty, where, we fear, it will be crushed by *wild beasts* at the approaching sessions of the respective Colonial Legislatures. . . . It is all very beautiful in theory to expatiate on the benefits of Colonial Federation. . . . This is all sublime and pleasing around a festive board; but of very little practical advantage to the people of our Island. We are part and parcel now of a greater nationality than can be scared up by even four millions of people for many a long day, we enjoy the protection of the government of that nation, railway communication will not likely ever come to our shores, and we have nothing worth sending to the top of Lake Superior; but as regards our lawyers and statesmen, we believe it would do some of them a vast of good to have an opportunity to know their own littleness, so far as this last consideration is concerned we go in heartily for a Confederation."

29 BRITISH ATTITUDES AS VIEWED BY BRITISH NORTH AMERICANS

Morning Telegraph, Saint John
Monday, September 12, 1864

An accurate representation of what British North Americans felt about British attitudes.

"Of one thing they [the British North American delegates at Charlottetown] ought to be satisfied, and that is that the Mother Country is becoming tired of her Colonial dependencies. This is undoubtedly the prevailing sentiment among the English Statesmen. — Veterans, like Lord Palmerston and Earl Derby may not say so, whatever they may feel; they leave the expression of such radical sentiments to the new school of politicians, to rising men of the stamp of Mr. Gladstone and Mr. Goldwin Smith . . . . It does not pay at present to retain the British North American Colonies. . . . Why, then, should the British take any special interest in our welfare. Blood goes for nothing these days, for Anglo-Saxon blood is everywhere. Commerce is everything — and everything must succumb to commercial calculations.

"We consider, then, that the time is near at hand when we shall be told to shift for ourselves; and the American difficulty, if we are not greatly mistaken, has brought the time considerably nearer to our doors than it otherwise would be."

30 SATIRICAL EXUBERANCE

Ross's Weekly, Charlottetown
Thursday, September 15, 1864

This delicious bit of overwriting was the result of criticisms in the Charlottetown Conservative papers of the way the local visiting circus had been fleecing the public, and of the kind of entertainment the circus offered. The grand ball, given by the Prince Edward Island government for the Charlottetown Conference delegates, on Thursday night, September 8, 1864, was an opportunity for John Ross, editor of *Ross's Weekly*, to get back at those who thought the Circus was immoral.

"A few days after the close of the circus, a great public 'Ball and Supper' is announced; the evening of the day arrives; the proud and the gay, arrayed in fashion's gauds, flock to the scene where revelry presides; the balls glow with gay trappings and gorgeous decorations; the lights are brilliant as the stars of heaven. Pleasure panoplied in lustful smiles meets and embraces exuberant Joy; the cup of passion is full to overflowing, and the devotee of pleasure hangs on the lip of delight

. . . . the fascinating dance goes merrily, and the libidi[n]ous waltz with its lascivious entwinements whiles in growing excitement; the swelling bosom and the voluptuous eye tell the story of the intemperate revel in the veins of the dancers. . . . In this scene, where intrigue schemes sin, and the libertine woes [*sic*] his victim, where the bold, lewd Bacchanal laughs, and lasciviousness reigns, our moralist mingles; here he rocks his piety to sleep, and cradles his morality in foregiveness; and the saint who could not tolerate satan in the circus, embraces the Prince of Darkness in the gilded scene of fashion's vices, and the reeking slough of debauchery."

31 THE CASE FOR CONFEDERATION

Morning Chronicle, Halifax
Thursday, September 22, 1864

This editorial suggests the hand of Jonathan McCully, one of the Nova Scotian delegates to Charlottetown and to Quebec, who had become an enthusiastic convert to Confederation in the process. He was also the editor of the Halifax *Morning Chronicle*, until the end of 1864.

"Select fifty men from the various Provinces — take them from the front rank and from all classes . . . and propound the question: Is the present condition of the British North American Provinces one which, in your opinion, is likely to continue as it is for all time coming?" 49 out of 50 would say no.

And no matter how the civil war ends, the United States, especially the northern part of it, "will emerge . . . chafed, angry and entertaining feelings of mortal hatred and revenge towards the Provinces. . . .

"Disjointed, disunited, with four or five mock Executives wholly independent of each other, what kind of a front, in our present organization, would we present to a foe? The condition we are in virtually seems to invite aggression. . . .

"Let these Provinces, however, be organized into one vast Confederation, with a central system of Executive Government and a quasi national character . . . we should soon possess all the prestige and command all the respect to which our numbers and our position would entitle us. . . .

"Our ships would be British American, our character, our position and our influence, would be known the world over, felt and respected."

32 THE WIT OF THE SATIRIST

Borderer, Sackville
Friday, March 17, 1865

A poetical satire on the seduction of the Charlottetown Conference by the Canadians.

. . . In secret conclave there they met,
With windows clos'd, doors barr'd
      they say.
And what they said, or what they did,
Has, to this day, been always hid.
But, in the midst of their confab,
A loud and thundering knock was
      heard,
Who's that who dares, cried one
      and all
To venture in this sacred hall,
Go, menials, go, and say to him,
By all the gods, he can't come in.
But as they stared in wild surprise,—
As if by magic, 'fore their eyes,
The door flew open, in there stalk'd,
Across the floor he boldly walk'd,
A Stranger, nor a word he said,
'Till he waved a hand o'er each
      one's head,
And then, in solemn tones and low,
These mystic words did from him flow,
"Multum plum pluribum presto*
Again he gravely waved his wand,
Adroitly slipping in the hand
Of each, among them as he pas'd,
A small and curious shap'd eye-glass,

Then on the floor he took his stand.
Anon, he waved his magic wand,
And thus, in thrilling tones but
      bland,
Address'd that honorable band:
"Illustrious Seigniors, it doth seem
To me a humbug this here Scheme**
But whether it be wrong or right,
I'll knock it higher than a kite,
And this is why I have come forth,
I am the Wizard of the North
When from my caldron fumes arise,
Then put your glasses to your eyes."
He paused, and instantaneously
Array'd in gorgeous robes was he,
His mien sublime, majestic, grand,
His wand and pot in either hand,
And lo! to their increas'd surprise,
Long wreaths of smoke began to rise,
—They clapped the glasses to their
      eyes —
In wisps, and twirls it did exhume,
And fragrant odors fill'd the room,
The Wizard vanished in the smoke,
From which these parting words he
      spoke,
"Seigniors adieu, I must not stay,
I'm off post-haste for Canada,
I summon you to haste away
And meet me there without delay."
To which the Seigniors, there and
      then,
Answer'd, in lusty tone, "Amen." . . .
Reader you know as well as I,
How there mid scenes of revelry,
At festive boards, at midnight balls,
With dance and song, in lordly halls,
How they caper'd with the Parlez-vous
Till they kick'd the buttons off
      their shoes,
Where'er they turned, on every hand,
They met the Wizard with his wand,
He sparkl'd in the ruby wine,
He glitter'd in the dresses fine,
He gleam'd 'neath tresses all divine
Of ladies fair, 'tis nonsurmise,
He fairly dazzled in their eyes.
Yet there amid these scenes they
      laid
The corner-stone of what they said,
Would make of us a mighty nation,
And christen'd it
"Confederation". . . .

The Quebec Conference

The Quebec Conference systematized and ratified what had already been suggested in broad outline at Charlottetown. This does not mean that the going was easy. It was not, at least, at first. The Senate — or Legislative Council as it was called at the time — created considerable difficulty. It was then believed — proved false soon enough after 1867 — that the Senate would be the main focus of British North American federalism, with its representation by regions, rather than, as in the House of Commons, by population. Edward Whelan was quite right in pointing out on Friday, October 14, that the crisis over the Senate threatened to break up the Conference when it was only five days old. But the question was solved by adhering to the original Charlottetown arrangement, and giving to Newfoundland (who had now joined the Conference) four senators for itself. Though other problems came, such as the House of Commons where Prince Edward Island wanted special consideration, none were quite so serious. Edward Palmer points this out in his letter to the Charlottetown *Monitor* of November 28. Of course, as Edward Whelan reveals time and again, the partying was continuous!

33 BRITAIN AND THE COLONIES: A PARTING OF THE WAYS?

Examiner, Charlottetown
Monday, October 31, 1864

The following is an excellent summary of opinions widely held in British North America about British feelings toward the Empire. The feelings of John Bull here sketched were, in fact, representative of an influential, articulate, and powerful segment of British opinion, led by the London *Times*.

"The people of Great Britain are now asking — Of what *use* are the Colonies? What return do we get for the three, four, and sometimes six millions annually spent upon them? What return do we get for the millions upon millions that they have already cost us? Are they not able to provide for their own defence? Is it fair that the over-taxed people of England should be still more over-taxed to provide for the defence of those who are, to all appearance, well able to defend themselves? . . . They argue that the Colonies would be just as available as fields for emigration, and that they would be quite as great consumers of articles of British manufacture, if they were independent States, as they now are in their subject condition. Old John Bull is heard to grumble somewhat after this fashion — 'Look at that great hulking fellow, Canada, and his smaller brothers, New Brunswick and Nova Scotia, with that impertinent, discontented little scoundrel, Prince Edward Island, are they going to be an everlasting expense to me? Must I be continually putting my hand in my pocket to keep them in fighting order? Only the other day, when their neighbour Jonathan doubled up his fists and looked fierce about that Trent affair, I was forced to shell out, I don't like to say how much money, to fit them for the ring. . . . They needn't expect me to fight their battles for them any longer: they must help themselves. If they choose still to board with me, well and good; I'll not turn them out of doors; but if they like better to go on their own hook, and set up house-keeping for themselves, why the sooner they do it the better for both of us, that's all I have to say.' Who can blame honest John for these mutterings? His reflections are those of every father who sees growing up around him a family of big, lazy boys, who are a great expense, and who seem unwilling to do anything towards their own support."

---

34 CONFEDERATION: FANTASY TURNS INTO REALITY

Intelligencer, Belleville
Friday, October 14, 1864

"This is the topic [Confederation] which now engrosses public attention. The petty game of provincial politics has given place to the nobler strife for a nationality. For years we have been talking of a Federal Union of the British Provinces, yet scarcely realizing what such a federation meant. It was an idea, but crude and undeveloped. It floated in our imagination more like a dream than a possible reality. It was something in the far-off future. . . . It was a relief to quit the muddy sea of politics and chat about the great nationality of which we only formed the embryo particles, but to witness with our eyes the inauguration of this great nationality was something beyond even our faintest anticipations. Back would we turn to the petty strifes and contentions which formed the staple product of our political warfare, waiting for something to turn up. . . .

"Amid the general despondency and gloom the scheme of Federation became the cynosure of attraction. It was that which would break the deadlock. . . . It was that which would lift us out of the slough, and under British sovereignty, make us a great nation."

---

35 DISAGREEMENT AMONG THE PROVINCES AT QUEBEC

Examiner, Charlottetown
Monday, October 24, 1864

Inter-Colonial Conference at Quebec, No. 2.

"Friday, 4 P.M., Oct. 14

"The Conference has just closed, and as the Mail for the Eastern Provinces will also close in a very short time, I may as well tell the readers of the *Examiner* some of the talk about town in regard to its deliberations. It is understood that the resolution regarding representation in the Upper House of the Confederate Parliament was debated all day with considerable warmth and ability, but no agreement come to. Lower Canada complains that in the number proposed for her — 24 — she would not be fairly represented — it being proposed that Upper Canada (against whom there is great jealousy) should have the same number, while the Maritime Provinces, it was proposed, should have thirty-two members. New Brunswick and Nova Scotia claim 22 members out of the 32, while Newfoundland and Prince Edward Island, it is supposed, will not be allowed to have more than 10 between them, which the representatives from those Islands will not agree to. And with so much diversity of opinion, it is very difficult to say whether the Convention will not be compelled to break up prematurely. Matters do not certainly look very promising for a completion of the deliberations. I hope there may be concession and reconciliation, but I have very grave doubts respecting a satisfactory result. The mail is just about closing. I hope to be able to give more cheering accounts in my next letter.

E. [dward] W. [helan]"

---

36 PLEASURE AT QUEBEC

Examiner, Charlottetown
Monday, October 31, 1864

The Inter-Colonial Conference at Quebec, No. 5.

"Quebec, Friday, Oct. 21

"It would seem to be the settled conviction of the good people of this gay, ancient, and fascinating City, that the chief end of existence is Pleasure. I am informed, however, that the season for paying particular devotion to this most exacting deity has not yet arrived — that winter, when the mighty river which pours its countless treasures into Lower Canada, is locked in the embrace of the Frost King — witnesses scenes of gaiety and festivity here to which those in which I have been a participator bear no comparison — at least for frequency of occurrence. May the good prayers of all our friends at home be copiously offered for us, to the end that we may be removed from this dear, charming, abominable, killing, pleasure ridden City, before the winter shall have set in, otherwise the probability is that the undertaker will effect our removal for us without our own volition.

"The Bachelors of Quebec gave a splendid Ball this evening, in honour of the Delegates, at the Parliament Buildings. . . . I shall not say anything more about the Ball. It was a brilliant affair throughout — eminently successful — (I believe that is the phrase used to describe a stunning jollification) — and Everybody and his Wife were hugely delighted with it. One word more: the Cabinet Ministers — the leading ones especially — are the most inveterate dancers I have ever seen; they do not seem to miss a dance during the live-long night. They are cunning fellows; and there's no doubt it is all done for a political purpose: they know that if they can dance themselves into the affections of the wives and daughters of the country, the men will certainly become an easy conquest."

---

37 FEDERAL DEBT ARRANGEMENTS

Examiner, Charlottetown
Saturday, October 22, 1864

"Canada proposes to deal with the Maritime Provinces in the most broad and liberal spirit. She emphatically declares that the burden of her debt shall fall upon Upper and Lower Canada — *and upon Upper and Lower Canada alone.* It is proposed to consolidate the debts of the several Provinces, the Confederation assuming their liability in consideration of the transfer of all provincial property of a public character — such as canals, public harbours, light houses, steamboats, dredges, and public vessels, river and lake improvements, railways, military, roads, public buildings, custom houses, and post offices, except such as may be set aside for the use of the local Legislatures; ordnance property, munitions of war, armories, and lands set apart for public purposes. The Confederation then proposes to place to the credit of each Province, to meet its debt, $25 per head of the population. If the debt of any one does not amount to that sum, that particular one can draw for the interest semi-annually. The debt of Canada is such that she will have nothing to draw — Nova Scotia and New Brunswick not much each — Newfoundland and Prince Edward Island will have a large balance in their favour."

---

38 ALLIANCE OF INTERESTS BETWEEN LOWER CANADA AND THE MARITIMES

Examiner, Charlottetown
Monday, November 7, 1864

The Inter-Colonial Conference at Quebec, No. 6.

"Thursday, October 27

"As it now appears to my mind, I have no reason, as far as the interests of the Island are concerned, to be dissatisfied with the arrangements proposed. Canada has, I think, shown a very honest and generous disposition so far; and should the Union be consummated, Lower Canada will, most especially, be the firm and fast friend of the Maritime Provinces. The desire of her public men is, apparently, to secure the aid of the Eastern Provinces for the purpose of curbing the grasping ambition of Upper or Western Canada, which now threatens to overshadow the Lower Province. The French desire most ardently to be left to the undisturbed enjoyment of their ancient privileges — their French institutions, civil law, literature and language. It is utterly impossible to Anglicise them — the attempt to do it, would outrage their most deeply rooted prejudices and lead to insurrec-·tion. As Sir Etienne Tache [*sic*] said to me to-day, (and he is a shrewd observer of events), the time will come — not, indeed, in the present generation, nor, perhaps, in the next — when the French element will be absorbed into the English one; but that result must be brought about by time, and not by the violent action of politicians. Leave to the French their old traditions, customs and institutions, and they will be found to be the most easily managed race in Canada under the British power."

39 THE COLONISTS IN COUNCIL

Gazette, Montreal
Friday, October 28, 1864 and Monday, October 31, 1864

Below is perhaps the best description ever penned of the Quebec Conference and its setting, by the Quebec correspondent of the Montreal *Gazette*. It was so popular at the time that the Montreal *Gazette* republished it three days later. It was also widely copied by other British North American papers, *e.g.*, the Halifax *Morning Chronicle*, November 5, 1864. It was in part the basis for W. M. Whitelaw's excellent article, "Reconstructing the Quebec Conference," *Canadian Historical Review*, June 1938. It is, however, quite long, and only sections can be given here.

"The Parliament buildings at Quebec are remarkable neither for beauty nor extent. Built to supply a temporary want, on the ruins of the stately 'palace of St. Louis,' they represent expediency rather than right. The shadow of Ottawa and the Queen's decision was upon them from the beginning, dwarfing and diminishing all their proportions. The very architect must have felt that he was bringing forth a posthumous child. . . . But if the plain and three storied building has nothing to recommend it, either to the eye or the understanding, the site on which it stands may challenge comparison with any in the world. Hewn out, halfway down the historic cliff, it is impossible to conceive a more commanding position. Hereabouts once stood the primitive frame-house and garden of Samuel Champlain, the founder of the city; and yonder, at the foot of the cliff, its last invader, Richard Montgomery, fell, on the last day of the memorable year 1776 [actually, Dec. 31, 1775]. Above, the citadel towers — the Gibraltar of the North. Below, Mountain-hill street dips down to the broad river, as steep as a stair of a timber slide. The grand battery buttresses the very walls. . . . In the wing of this homely edifice, so splendidly surrounded. . . . [is the reading room of the Legislative Council where the Conference met.]

[Taché]: "Under a refinement of manners only too unusual in this age, he concealed a latent fire and determination of character."

[Tupper]: "forcible, keen and emphatic . . . a suppressed temptation to sarcasm in his tones. . . . "

[Tilley]: " . . . without having the extraordinary facility which on such subjects [financial] that distinguishes Mr. Galt, he was always clear, cogent and to the point. The unpardonable sin in Mr. Tilley's mind, would seem to be, surplusage. . . He possesses above most of his colleagues that essential knowledge for a good party leader, the knowledge of where and when *to stop*. Any ordinary man can open an argument; most men can keep one up, but Mr. Tilley always knows where his matter ends. . . . And the condensation of his style is no bad index to the tenacity of his character. To carry his points was his all in all, and it is but justice to him to say, he generally succeeded. . . . "

[Editorial]:

"But what was most remarkable of all was that these men, all bred in small communities, and raised to positions of influence amid the contests of jarring petty factions, showed complete forgetfulness of all personal difference, all local distinctions, and spoke as they acted (we have reason to believe) at Quebec, with a large-hearted patriotism which it warmed one's heart to witness. Will the people follow the example, and rise to the level of the occasion — to settle now the destiny of this northern country, and the people that dwell here . . . ?"

40 NOVA SCOTIAN REACTIONS TO THE RESULTS OF THE QUEBEC CONFERENCE

British Colonist, Halifax
Tuesday, November 22, 1864

The Halifax *British Colonist* reflected Tupper and the Conservative administration of Nova Scotia, in power since 1863. This editorial reflects something also of the character of the Quebec Conference.

"Something had to be done: *viz.*, a Union of the Colonies had to be brought about. We assume that there is no question upon that. We feel assured that the necessity for that Union is conceded by every loyal and intelligent British American. What remained to be done was to decide upon what terms the Union could be effected. . . . What the delegates on the Quebec Conference had to provide for was, first, a strong Central Government, a sufficiently firm consolidation of the Provinces to insure their acting as an undivided and indivisible unit *in all cases where necessary*. But British America comprises a vast territory, embracing a diversity of races in its population, and also a diversity of clearly marked and localized public institutions recognized by existing laws. Common justice required that some guarantees should be provided for the preservation of vested rights. . . . Therefore, the delegates had to provide, secondly, for the due protection and management of exclusively local interests, without prejudice to the country as a whole. Whilst doing this, it was necessary to guard against the absurdity of allowing any local political divisions to imagine themselves 'sovereign states' — of making, in short, our Union a mere political partnership, dissolvable at the pleasure of any of its members . . . .

"The provision for the constitution of the General Parliament and of the subordinate legislatures, is of the very essence of the scheme we are discussing. It is in this that they have, as we contend, outlined a Constitution more nearly perfect than any that was ever yet previously framed."

---

41 FEARS OF PALMER CONCERNING PRINCE EDWARD ISLAND AND FEDERATION

Monitor, Charlottetown
Thursday, December 15, 1864

Quotation from a letter by Edward Palmer from Quebec, dated October 21, 1864.

"The scheme of a Federal Government is making progress, and I have no doubt will be agreed to by a large majority of the delegates; but I regret to say, from all that is developed so far, I fear our little Island is to be sacrificed. The Canadian ministers or their leaders are clever and ingenious men. They are in this position: their government must stand or fall in the accomplishment or failure of the Union. . . . The great principles I may, however, say, are pretty nearly decided on, and secondary principles are details now under discussion. These are as you may imagine, the most difficult to adjust: but still I think a scheme will be agreed to, and if it turns out to be what it promises at present, I hope *most earnestly,* and I have no doubt, that our Legislature will discard it. . . . The paltry proportion of representation we are *now* likely to have in both branches of the [central] Legislature is little more than nominal, and leaves us at the mercy of the other Provinces. . . . In short, I am throroughly [*sic*] disgusted at the course things have taken here and would be disposed to 'sit by the waters of Babylon and weep' for years, if I thought our Island people would be taken in by the scheme."

42 THE CURRENT SETS WITH THE CANADIANS

Monitor, Charlottetown
Saturday, December 3, 1864

Letter from Edward Palmer dated November 28, 1864.

"For the first few days [of the Quebec Conference] the leading delegates of the Lower Provinces exhibited caution and vigilance upon every question affecting the interests of these Provinces, and in debate on any proposition met the Canadian ministers with adequate ability. As the business proceeded, and the details of the federal union were from day to day laid down, parties evinced a visible elasticity of judgement, and were observed gradually to harmonize with those whose opinions they had previously met in a style more polemical in character. The current seemed to set with the Canadians. The maritime delegates, one after the other, were observed to drop into the stream; and, with few exceptions, the members of the Conference appeared to float along with it, scarcely producing a ripple on its now gentle surface. . . . Let the Union take place if the other Maritime Colonies think it in their interest to go into it. Should the change, after a sufficient trial, be decidedly successful, this Island may consent to join it. . . . "

---

43 ANOTHER VIEW OF THE QUEBEC CONFERENCE

Halifax Citizen, Halifax
Saturday, November 19, 1864

Many and varied were the Maritime satires on secrecy and the partying of the Quebec Conference. Probably both were essential, but to make fun of them was irresistible for anti-Confederates. One of the most amusing was *Barney Rooney's letters on Confederation, Botheration and Political Transmogrification*, which were published in the *Halifax Citizen*, November 19 to December 31, 1864. They were later republished as a pamphlet. (Tilley, by the way, was a temperance advocate.)

"So whin the dellygates got dark afther a hard day's conspirocy, and D'Arcy [McGee] rang fur light [rum] and lemons, fair it's rate and aisy Terry slipped into the room [Terry being a 13th cousin of McGee's], and was snug as a hare in a cabbage row upon a mountain iv champagne baskets in a corner. . . .

John A. [Macdonald]: 'but hand us the tipple iv ye iver stop suppin' to see iv it's strong enough; an' toss a lemon to Tilley, the sowl, iv he must do penance like a patriarch.'

'I'll hae whuskey,' sez Jarge [Brown], '. . . my certie, ye're richt though, Darcie lad, aboot the danger o' gangin' ower early tae the polls. We ken better than the people what's guid for them. . . . Dinna ye think sae, Mister Crupper?'

'Sir,' sez Tupper, as he dried the bottom iv his tumbler, and held it handy to D'Arcy's ladle, 'the well understood wishes iv the people are so notirously in favor iv this scheme that it would be a reckless and infamous policy to put them to the trouble of expressing themselves in a special vote upon it. . . . My dear McCully, I am sure you will agree with me. . . . '

'My dear Tupper,' sez McCully, 'yes — no — that is, I mean yes, — or rather no; but I want to see you privately about it. . . . '

Och, thin, its mad enough and merry enough their Conference grew; Brown dancing 'Tulloch gonem' to a ballad from Darcy . . . and the rest clinking glasses every second or two, till Tilly got the hiccup wid the sour lemmons he sucked, and tryin' to light his bed room candle put out the gas and fell over the manly figger iv Cartier under the table — and after that ye needn't wait to be towld that there was a yelp in French and a howlin' scrimmage. . . . "

B. Colonial reactions to the Quebec Resolutions

The Quebec Conference appears to have decided that wherever possible it was desirable to avoid elections on the Confederation issue. This policy worked in the Province of Canada and in Nova Scotia, where elections had been held in 1863, and there was no need, at least not technically, for elections until the summer of 1867. In Canada there was little pressure for an election, and Cartier, Macdonald, and Brown had no intention of calling one. In Nova Scotia it was different. There was tremendous pressure for an election, but Tupper was determined to avoid one, so long as he could count on a working majority in the Assembly. As it turned out he was able to hang onto power until Confederation was achieved in 1867. Then, and only then, was there a Nova Scotian election, and Tupper's party was then resoundingly defeated. But by then it was too late.

This policy was not possible in New Brunswick. The last election had been held early in 1862. The question there was simply deciding when was the best time to have one. It was actually held in February and March, 1865; and to the dismay of Canadians, and of Confederation supporters in Nova Scotia, Tilley and those who supported Confederation were defeated. This explains the uneasy, what-shall-we-do-now, tone in the Canadian newspapers in the spring and early summer of 1865.

In Prince Edward Island an election would have made little difference. It soon became obvious that the Island was opposed to union in any form, whether Maritime union or British North American federal union, and an election, one way or the other, would have made little difference. There was an election in February, 1867, and it put the Liberals into power. They were more opposed to Confederation than the Conservatives they replaced. In Newfoundland there was an election in November, 1865, but it, too, made no substantial difference in prospects for Confederation.

In assessing the newspaper discussion of Confederation it is useful to remember that ideas and editorials were used as political weapons. There was, for example, the argument that Confederation being a federal union, would be sowed with the seeds of its own dissolution.

Federation, in other words, was a thoroughly bad principle for any union. This was a lesson that many had read from the American Civil War. The argument from it was used by anti-Confederates both in Nova Scotia and New Brunswick. The supporters of Confederation replied to this argument. They said that Confederation might be called "federal," but it had many centralizing devices specifically designed to overcome the basic weakness of federation, a weakness that American experience had demonstrated so clearly. Thus suspicion of federation appears on both sides of the Confederation issue.

There were others, however, who opposed Confederation because they believed it was too highly centralized — that it was legislative union in all but name. This argument appeared among French-Canadian newspapers opposed to Confederation, and to some extent also in New Brunswick, as well as in a few Reform papers in Canada West who had refused to accept the Coalition of 1864. Broadly the argument here was that the local provincial governments under the new constitution would be such cardboard and paste affairs that they could be knocked down whenever the central government felt like it.

Once these various positions are understood, it then becomes clear why the Nova Scotian opposition, for example, damned Confederation as a federal system, leaving the impression that they might have accepted a British North American legislative union. It is highly doubtful they would have done any such thing. Any stick to beat Confederation with was handy, and since that argument was popular it was used.

Canada West

Canada West was strongly behind Confederation. At one stroke all the grievances voiced, all the reforms urged by Canada West for a decade past, were incorporated into one grand reform. "Rep. by pop." would come in the shape of a central House of Commons. In addition, Canada West could look forward to her own provincial Assembly to spend provincially raised taxes on provincial objects, such as education.

The Toronto *Globe* was a great supporter of this movement, and most of the Reform journals followed. Conservative newspapers were a little less comfortable, but by and large were prepared to follow Macdonald and accept Confederation. What is interesting is the unease that developed in the spring and early summer of 1865 after the defeat of Confederation and Tilley in the New Brunswick election. Moreover, Canada West was also extremely uncomfortable about the United States. That country was chafed and angry over a number of issues, both with Great Britain and with British North America. This raised in an acute form anxieties about Canadian defence. Was in fact any defence against the United States possible?

By mid-summer 1865, some of this unease had dissipated. Anxiety about the United States was to continue, though it shifted to new ground by early 1866, that is, fear of a Fenian invasion. However, the Colonial Office in London made known new and, for Confederation supporters, encouraging directives. As early as December, 1864, the British Government had strongly approved of Confederation; a dispatch to the governors of the Atlantic colonies, on June 24, 1865, made it very clear that the British Government not only approved Confederation, but

for the sake of defence and other reasons, was going to insist upon it. This was to have real results in the spring of 1866, when the anti-Confederate Smith government of New Brunswick was turned out of office by the Lieutenant-Governor, and a new government, sympathetic to Confederation, was brought in.

44 FEDERATION DIFFERS FROM THE UNITED STATES SYSTEM

Globe, Toronto
Monday, August 1, 1864

"We sometimes meet the objection to the federation scheme that that form of government has proved a failure in the United States. We do not believe that it has. We have always held that the Civil War . . . is due to a cause quite unconnected with the federal character of its government. . . .

"The civil war, it is quite true, has afforded an excellent opportunity of judging the weak points and defects in the United States constitution. It has especially shown the evil which the 'States-rights' doctrine involves. The idea of the United States constitution is that the central government is a delegated government, deriving its powers from the 'sovereign' States which go to make up the Union . . . . the policy of those who have taken in hand to apply the federal principle in this country, is directly the reverse of that adopted by the framers of the United States constitution. They propose that the local governments shall be the delegated governments. . . . "

45 FEDERATION: A SYSTEM BEST SUITED TO CANADIAN DIVERSITY

Oshawa Vindicator, Oshawa
Wednesday, August 31, 1864

This is the type of argument in favour of federation that might have been expected everywhere, and is, in fact, encountered only rarely.

"No system of Government could be fairer, or could be better calculated to give satisfaction to all parties interested, than the federal system. In speaking thus we do not wish to be understood as advocating the adoption of the details of federation as it has been carried out in the neighbouring Union, for we believe that although the system in vogue in the United States does infinite credit to the men who first brought it into being, yet time has shown wherein it may be improved upon. . . But of the two systems of Government, the Legislative and the Federal, there is no doubt whatever in our mind as to which would be found to work satisfactorily, and which would tend to produce discord and discontent in, at least, some sections of the contemplated union. The Legislative union works very well in England, with Parliament assembled under the eye of Her Majesty, and representing so small a territory. But with such diverse interests as would be brought together in a British American union extending eventually over the whole of British North America, a system of Government more like that under which the United States has grown to such vast proportions is what is plainly required in order to do justice to the varied and widely separated interests involved."

46 RESERVATIONS WITH REGARD TO FEDERATION

Spectator, Hamilton
Monday, October 31, 1864

"We need not repeat how much we regret that this [Federal union] should have been so: but it is some satisfaction to know that there were not wanting men in the [Quebec] Conference strongly wedded to the idea of a simple legislative Union, and thoroughly alive to the dangers of the federal system. . . .

"The first principle of the new Constitution is that the Central Government shall be, under the Crown, absolute and supreme in the country. Give us the details to work out fairly that idea, and we care not whether the Union is called federal or legislative, except as to the mere matter of expense. A strong supreme central government, delegating to the local legislatures certain powers for the management and control of local interests and objects, even controlling their action so as to protect the rights of minorities in each section, and reserving to itself absolute and unchecked control of all subjects not so specially delegated, is certainly the simplest and most innocent form in which the 'federal' principle could be presented to us. The local Parliaments exercising these functions by virtue of the privileges thus delegated to them, present a vastly different thing from the State Legislatures of the American union. . . . ."

47 WAR CLOUDS AND CONFEDERATION

Morning Telegraph, Saint John
Friday, December 30, 1864

Letter from their Quebec correspondent.

On December 14, 1864, the Confederate "raiders" who had held up the banks in St.

Alban's, Vermont, two months before, and had been arrested by Canadian detectives, were discharged by a Montreal magistrate, C. J. Coursol, for want of jurisdiction. This had tremendous repercussions in Washington. General J. A. Dix of New York ordered American troops to pursue any other raiders right into Canada, if necessary, and under no circumstances to surrender them to Canadian authorities, but return them to New York for trial under martial law. On December 17, the State Department required passports for all British North Americans travelling to the United States. There was also talk of ending the bonding privilege for Canadian goods travelling to and from American ports. Notice was given in January, 1865, about the ending of the Reciprocity Treaty, effective the following year. These events, in their turn, had considerable effects in British North America, and particularly, in the Province of Canada.

"Canada is just now awaking to a knowledge that in the winter season she is wholly at the mercy of the American people for communication with Europe. . . . Under these circumstances it is only natural and proper that the Inter-Colonial Railroad should occupy the first place in the thoughts of Canadian merchants and politicians. . . . I should judge that if the threats of the [United States] Federal Government be suspended over the heads of the Canadians until Parliament assemble here [on January 19, 1865], it will not take that body twenty-four hours to give in its adhesion of the leading principles of the Confederation Scheme. Men will scarcely stop to *think* when war clouds are rolling over the land; they will ACT, — and that quickly. The demand for an appeal to the people will scarcely be heard, and certainly will be unheeded."

48 VITALITY OF THE FEDERATION ISSUE IN THE MARITIMES

Intelligencer, Belleville
Friday, January 20, 1865

"It is somewhat remarkable that while we in Canada have said very little, written very little, or thought very little about the details of the Confederation scheme, the Maritime Provinces have been agitated from centre to circumference. — Scarcely had the Delegates returned to their homes [after the Quebec Conference], before party lines were down with a distinctness which clearly marked the friends and opponents of the measure. In every township, village, town and city, public meetings were held, and the subject in all its details thoroughly discussed. . . . "

49 BRITISH AMERICAN ATTITUDES TO GOVERMENT AND SOCIETY

Evening Journal, St. Catharines
Wednesday, February 22, 1865

There is a solid ring of authenticity about this assessment, by a Reform paper be it noted, of Canadian attitudes to government and society. It also represents widely-held views in British North America generally.

"We don't desire our institutions to be the playthings of an irresponsible Executive, or the footballs of a senseless and levelling rabble, or the targets for wide-mouthed fanatics to shoot their mad ravings at. We are not money or title worshippers, but we believe that property has rights which should not be ignored and that the constitution which makes the *vox populi* the 'all in all', political or governmental power has an inherent weakness which must result in its own death. . . .

"The freedom of the subject, and the rights of property — the well-grounded distinctions which exist in all societies between man and man — those social distinctions which are observed in every community — the intellectual and other differences which exist between peoples — we intend to recognize as far as possible in our new Constitution. . . . The British Ameri-

94

cans have known the defects of the American system of government for years, and have determined to follow a better model in their new Constitution."

50 TWO VIEWS OF THE QUEBEC DEBATES

Leader, Toronto
Wednesday, January 25, 1865

Two reports of the debates at Quebec. Parliament opened on January 19, 1865. The Confederation debate began, in the Legislative Council, on February 3. This first report is from the *Leader's* Quebec correspondent of January 21, 1865.

"There is a perfect lull to-day in the political atmosphere, and hardly a single subject is to be found upon which to hang a letter worth reading. This is the third day of the session and we haven't had a fight yet. Politics are at a discount . . . Quebec, as far as politics are concerned, is in a sort of lethargic sleep, the depth of which it is impossible to fathom, and the profundity of which makes one despair of ever 'seeing life' again . . . . the social world of Quebec cannot be said to be in the same condition. . . . "

Tuesday, February 28, 1865

"[There are reasons for] the irredeemable dullness of the debate. Set speeches, unless in very skilful hands, are very much like stale small beer, of which the effervesence has been lost before it is used. . . . The zest of personal interest in the debate is wholly wanting. Nobody says anything he was not expected to say; there is nobody to be convinced, for every vote was pretty well predetermined. The fate of a Ministry does not hang upon a question on which a large majority of the House are known to be ready to vote with the yeas. Nothing comes to relieve the tedium;

and it is evident that members turn with a relish from this standing dish of unrelieved dullness, to the superior excitement which a small railroad bill can be made to yield. . . . We are doomed to be Confederated; and there is no good reason why the agony of suspense should be cruelly protracted."

51 A FURTHER VIEW OF THE CONFEDERATION DEBATE AT QUEBEC

Stratford Beacon, Stratford
Friday, March 3, 1865

Report of its Quebec correspondent of February 25, 1865.

"The Confederation debate has been voted a bore from the commencement. It drags its slow length along at the rate of about three hours a day. The members have all made up their minds how they will vote, and there is not a feature of the scheme which will be changed by any amount of oratory. The whole thing is a foregone conclusion, and hon. members who are to be met with in the library, in the reading-room, in the smoking room, or in the saloon — for the saloon is still an 'institution' of the House in spite of the resolution which was passed some time ago for its abolishment — are prepared to endure anything rather than listen to set speeches."

52 WHICH COURSE SHOULD CANADA ADOPT?

Prescott Telegraph, Prescott
Wednesday, March 8, 1865

"The question now very naturally arises, what will Canada do if, as is all but certain, the New Brunswick Legislature rejects Confederation . . . .

Whether in the event of Nova Scotia agreeing, our government would be willing to be united with that Province and Newfoundland, leaving New Brunswick and Prince Edward's Island out in the cold; or whether they would refuse to do this and fall back on the plan for a federation of Upper and Lower Canada alone, or further, whether they would rather break up the whole scheme and allow us quietly to drift into the Union on the other side of the St. Lawrence, which the Premier and several other equally distinguished members of our legislature declare is our inevitable fate, unless a Confederate union among ourselves is consummated, are questions which the future alone can answer."

53 SETBACK FOR UNION

Globe, Toronto
Friday, March 24, 1865

The defeat of Tilley and Confederation in the New Brunswick election of March, 1865, unhinged the Confederation movement. The best Tupper was able to do in the Nova Scotian Assembly was to renew a resolution for Maritime union. There are signs of impatience in the Reform party of Canada.

"The great Confederation, we have no doubt, will come, and possibly may work more harmoniously in consequence of the delay in its accomplishment. But it is impossible to conceal from ourselves that this action on the part of Nova Scotia is a fresh indication that the larger union is a thing of the future, not of the present, and it seems to us that our Government will be speedily called upon to adopt a new policy. . . . It is impossible that Canada can delay its constitutional reforms for an indefinite period."

54 CANADIAN VULNERABILITY IN THE FACE OF POSSIBLE UNITED STATES AGGRESSION

Evening Times, Hamilton.
In the London Evening Advertiser
Wednesday, March 15, 1865

"We cannot afford to have the spectacle of Denmark [i.e., the Schleswig-Holstein war, 1864] played over again. . . . Another conclusion that has been arrived at, is that in no case will Canadians consent to take part in a war of which the issue would be, to them, hopeless defeat."

Evening Times, Hamilton.
In the London Evening Advertiser
Saturday, March 18, 1865

"Are we going too far when we say there does not exist in the world a country more ineligible for defensive purposes than Canada? We are all frontier, and are open to attack at almost every point of that frontier . . . . Inherently strong, and armed and equipped at every point, the United States stands forth a giant encased in armor. What would our prospects be should we come into collision with this power?"

55 FEAR OF SEVERANCE OF LINKS WITH BRITAIN

Northern Advance, Barrie
Wednesday, July 5, 1865

"It is useless to attempt to disguise the fact that we are just now passing through a crisis, the end of which it is impossible to foresee. . . . The tone of some of the leading journals in England, and the language of many of her politicians, has been far from reassuring. . . . Let the policy of cutting her colonies adrift, and snubbing them if they appear unwilling to go, be adopted by England, and the dismemberment of the empire will soon be followed by loss of *prestige* and of power. . . .

"It is the duty of the parent to protect the child, and, in so far as defence is concerned, this Province is little past infancy. We are, no doubt, willing to bear a share of the burden, but all that lies in our power is but of little account. If England shall have said to our delegates, 'Canada must defend herself, or pay the cost of doing so', it would be tantamount to a declaration, that she wished the connection to end, and only wanted a pretext for forcing the accomplishment of that object. . . . In another generation or two Canada, or the British Confederate Provinces might be fairly considered old and strong enough to take an independent stand amongst the nations; and in doing so would, no doubt, retain toward England that feeling of affection which will always be felt towards one who has proved a generous protector, but let the connection be rudely or selfishly severed now, or before we are prepared for a change, and no such feeling can be expected to remain."

---

56 A CHANGED SITUATION

Stratford Beacon, Stratford
Friday, September 28, 1866

Report of McGee's address at London, C. W., of September 20.

"I do not say it is all plain sailing even now; but when I look back two short years, and remember that it was only in September, 1864, the first actual overture was made at the Conference at Charlottetown. . . . Friendly relations were established between the press of all the Provinces, until to-day our papers discuss their affairs, and they discuss ours almost as habitually as they do their own local affairs. (Cheers.) This is very different from the state of

things in 1862. — when I became President of the Council [in the Sandfield Macdonald government], and found, to my amazement, that even the Executive Council of Canada had not a single Lower Province paper on its fyles, except, as well as I remember, the old weekly *Nova Scotian*.*"

*The *Nova Scotian* was a weekly edition of the Halifax *Morning Chronicle*.

---

57 MACDONALD AND FEDERAL UNION

Citizen, Ottawa
Friday, September 29, 1865

Part of Macdonald's speech at a luncheon the previous day.

"Just as sure as I address you, sir, so sure will all the Provinces of British North America be united. . . . We shall see it before another year has passed. You may read in the papers about obstructions in one colony or another, but I do not speak incautiously . . . when I say that the union of all the Provinces is a fixed fact. . . . The mere struggle for office and fight for position — the differences between the 'outs' and the 'ins' have no charms for me; but now I have something worth fighting for — and that is the junction of Her Majesty's subjects in all British North America as one great nation. . . . "

Canada East

Before the results of the Charlottetown and Quebec Conferences were in any way known, a debate developed in Canada East between French-Canadian Conservative papers and English-Canadian ones, over what the new federal constitution should be. *La Minerve* of Montreal, for example, which usually reflected Cartier, went much beyond what the Canadian ministers were in fact prepared to do, in giving power to the future provincial governments.

When the Quebec Resolutions were published, they appeared first, and perhaps significantly in a French-Canadian paper that supported Confederation, *Le Journal de Québec,* on November 8, 1864. French-Canadian opposition papers accused the Conservative ministers of having betrayed French-Canadian interests. Confederation, said A. A. Dorion, was nothing else than a legislative union disguised with the name "federal." French-Canadian institutions were in his view by no means safe under such a constitution. French-Canadian government papers, like *Le Courrier du Canada,* insisted that adequate guarantees existed, and that the new constitution was to all intents and purposes federal.

The opposition papers in 1865 even talked about annexation as giving better security for French-Canadian institutions than Confederation. This however was short-lived. The Fenian crises of June, 1866, and afterwards, when Canada was forced to defend both the Niagara border and the French-Canadian border, against Fenian attacks, seriously weakened French-Canadian opposition to Confederation. *Mandements* from French-Canadian bishops, in June, 1867, urging acceptance of Confederation did the rest.

58 CONFEDERATION: THE ONLY ANSWER

Le Canadien, Quebec
Monday, August 1, 1864 [translation]

"Democratic newspapers and *Le Pays*

[of Montreal] in particular pretend to confuse federation, i.e. the federation of the two Canadas, with the confederation of all the British provinces. It is important, however, to distinguish between the two systems, one of which is only a temporary and debatable answer to the difficulties created by the Union, while the other is the most acceptable solution for our future that politicians have yet been able to devise. . . .

"In brief, do we have any other future alternative than annexation to the United States or the confederation of all the states of British North America?"

59 LEGISLATIVE UNION RATHER THAN FEDERAL UNION

Gazette, Montreal
Wednesday, August 24, 1864

"[The Toronto *Globe*] . . . says that if any union is determined on at Charlottetown it will be a legislative one. This is doubtless the opinion derived from contact with the leading men of the Acadian Provinces. And we believe that the tendency of public opinion also since Parliament was prorogued has been decidedly in the same direction. An absolute, complete legislative union is perhaps impossible. We are much inclined to think that it is. But reaping instruction from the pregnant example of our neighbours — Canadians and Acadians alike will infuse as little of federal principle into their union when established as will suffice to meet the absolute necessities of the case."

60 FEDERALISM: A PROTECTION OF FRENCH-CANADIAN INTERESTS

La Minerve, Montreal
Tuesday, August 30, 1864 [translation]

This is *La Minerve's* reply to the *Gazette's* editorial of August 24, 1864. The firm positions taken by each of these two Conservative newspapers was in the absence of any definitive statement by the Canadian cabinet. Semi-official statements were issued shortly after the Charlottetown Conference.

"The *Gazette* is certainly mistaken if it believes that public opinion in Lower Canada is in favour of a legislative union. On the contrary French Canadians will always be most strongly opposed to this measure because they see in it the destruction of their nationality.

"We want a confederation in which the federal principle would be applied as widely as possible, one which would leave the central government control of general questions only and in no way affect the interests of each separate section, and which would hand over to the individual local legislatures all responsibility for private interests. We wish each state to be completely independent of the others in matters concerning its own existence. . . .

"The central authority will be sovereign without doubt, but it will have competence only in certain general areas to be well defined in the constitution."

61 SUPPORT FOR A LEGISLATIVE UNION

Gazette, Montreal
Friday, September 2, 1864

"[The editorial of August 24th has] . . . produced a great deal of comment and some earnest protests. It seems almost to have excited alarm in some quarters. . . . We said then, and we repeat it now, that any union between these colonies must be, as nearly as possible, a legislative union. . . . We reassert these as fundamental principles on which the union must be based. . . . Let us have a union likely to last, and to not break down like that of our neighbors from innate defects — or let us have none at all. . . . All know the imperfections of the federal bond of union — the great difficulties which arise out of its complexity. History teems with them. When such a machine is set in motion, there must be some controlling influence; either centripetal power tending to consolidation, or centrifugal tending to separation."

"[However, because of the French Canadians as well as the great diversities of the country] . . . we would accept such an admixture of the Federal principle as would satisfy the just claims of French Canadians, — but not one whit more."

62 WHAT FEDERATION MUST NOT BE

True Witness and Catholic Chronicle, Montreal
Friday, September 23, 1864

Of all the Canadian papers, the Montreal *True Witness* had the shrewdest grasp of the principles of a federal system applied to British North America. This was owing almost entirely to a brilliant editor, G. E. Clerk, brought to Montreal to edit the English Roman Catholic paper by Bishop Bourget.

"Our position is this: that repeal of the existing union betwixt Upper and Lower Canada, and restoration to both of their respective legislatures and autonomy is the indispensable preliminary to any Federation . . . without which, in short, Federation is not possible or even conceivable.

"Therefore it is that we oppose the proposed plan of *Colonial* Federation, since no matter in what terms it may be conceived, it proposes to saddle us with a sovereign central government which in our actual position must derive its authority not from within, or from the States over which it is to bear rule; but *ab extra,* and from an Imperial Government with which our connection must cease ere many years be past; and to which, and to the plenitude of whose authority the said central government would then inevitably succeed. Our position [in Canada East] would then be that of a subject Province, not that of a State or independent member of a Confederation."

63 PROVINCIAL RIGHTS AND FEDERALISM

Le Courrier du Canada, Quebec
Monday, October 10, 1864 [translation]

"Let us give to each province its own distinct autonomy, let each province be master in its own house in matters of social organisation, ownership of public property, preservation of its language, laws and institutions, while protecting minorities everywhere, and let us unite all the parts into a federal agreement covering matters in which a common defence and common interests see us all joined on the same ground."

64 FEDERALISM: ANOTHER NAME FOR LEGISLATIVE UNION?

Le Pays, Montreal
Tuesday, November 8, 1864 [translation]

This is part of A. A. Dorion's address to the electors of Hochelaga, November 7, 1864.

"But in order for there to be confederation the different states must be linked to each other for matters of general interest, yet preserving their own independence for everything relating to their internal government. For what sort of independence will the various provinces keep under the proposed constitution, with a central government exercising a sovereign authority not merely in measures of common interest but even more over the bulk of the acts of local legislatures! [*i.e.* through disallowance]. What independence will they keep if they are deprived of the right to regulate their criminal laws, their commercial laws. . . . if they don't even have the right to determine the set-up of their law courts or to name the judges who will have to watch over the carrying out of the laws?

"It is thus not a confederation that has been proposed to us, but simply a legislative union disguised under the name of confederation."

65 CONFEDERATION, X

Le Courrier du Canada, Quebec
Monday, December 26, 1864 [translation]

"The most important point, we would go so far as to say the only important point of the constitutional scheme is assuredly the one defining the respective competences of the federal and local governments. That is the key, the foundation of the constitution . . . [The constitution gives] local governments sufficient guarantees to protect them against any attempt at trespass on the part of the central government, and it gives the central government a sufficient number of powers to enable it to work without harrassment for the national welfare and the betterment of the different states of the confederation, collectively and individually."

66 A EUROPEAN VIEW OF FEDERALISM

L'Ordre, Montreal
Monday, January 2, 1865 [translation]

"We publish without comment the following article on confederation by Mr. Rameau. We are pleased that our evaluations coincide so perfectly. . . . [The following cited from Paris *L'Economiste Français*, December 8, 1864.] . . . 'Every federal organisation which is not in principle strictly limited so as to be more than a common meeting ground, such as the German Diet, is always impelled forward by the logic of things and its own natural impetus to become the dominant power and more and more to overwhelm all local powers. . . . Thus it is of prime necessity to limit federal authority, tightly and in advance, and to leave it practically no financial or military strength, as is the case in Germany'. . . . "

67 A FRENCH-CANADIAN VIEW OF THE NECESSITY OF CHANGE

La Minerve, Montreal
Saturday, February 18, 1865 [translation]

"Canada's situation is quite exceptional. But if the dangers are great, if we absolutely must assume the expense of an army and an intercolonial railway, if we are to avoid eventual annexation and seek new markets for our products [as a result of the ending of the Reciprocity Treaty] a happy coincidence enables us to obtain all these results without ruining our financial position nor endangering a single one of our national rights. But these circumstances will not last for ever."

68 CHANGE HAS TO COME

Gazette, Montreal
Friday, March 3, 1865

The Montreal *Gazette* is replying to a number of points raised by Christopher Dunkin in his famous speech against Confederation in the Canadian Assembly, February 27 and 28, 1865.

"He must be a sanguine man who thinks that, after an acknowledgement that Upper Canada is entitled, according to population, to 17 more members than Lower Canada, the agitation can ever again be quelled."

69 CONFEDERATION AND AMERICAN CONFEDERATION

L'Ordre, Montreal
Wednesday, June 7, 1865 [translation]

"We have no hesitation in saying and maintaining that from all points of view, our institutions, our language and our laws will be better protected in an American confederation than in the scheme for the confederation of the provinces of British North America."

Friday, June 9, 1865 (above article continued)
"Ask businessmen, farmers, professional men, even the clergy, the response will be the same: 'Rather than exhaust our people by vast, insufficient expenditures on defence, rather than expose the country to all the disasters of a war we are certain to lose, rather than see our trade and agriculture paralysed by the abrogation of the Reciprocity Treaty, rather than see our institutions, our language, our laws at the mercy of a hostile majority in the central Parliament of the confederation scheme where the French element will be in a five to one minority, we prefer to enter into negotiations with our neighbouring confederation and in a friendly manner settle the conditions

for our entry as a sovereign state into the American Union.' "

70 LOWER CANADA'S FEAR OF OUTSIDE DECISIONS

Le Canadien, Quebec
Friday, May 18, 1866 [translation]

Le Canadien's fear was of "l'arbitrage impérial," that is, changes in the Quebec Resolutions to make them more acceptable to the Maritime provinces by a conference sitting in London, and whose work would at once be translated into an Imperial Act. This issue was to be much mitigated, two weeks after the editorial below by the Fenian invasions of June, 1866.

"At the outset of this discussion [it had gone on for two weeks] we said that the Canadian government was the chief author of the policy now being relentlessly pushed in the Maritime Provinces which has for its goal '*imperial arbitration.*' We accused our ministers of betraying us and of wanting to put the rights of Lower Canada at the mercy of a convention sitting in London, deliberating under the influence of the Colonial Office, and whose decisions would be without appeal."

71 A CHANGE OF VIEW

L'Ordre, Montreal
Wednesday, June 6, 1866 [translation]

A quite different attitude is evident in *L'Ordre* after the Fenian invasion at Ridgway June 1 and 2, 1866. The following poem, "Aux Militaires de la Campagne" is symptomatic.

"Yesterday still, dwellers on the land,
Living at peace under quiet roofs,
The woodsman climbing the mountain
  slopes,
To fell the trees of the forest groves.

But today shouts of 'blood' and 'war'
Echo under the vault of heaven above!
Take leave then of your father
Your friends and the mother you love.

Tear yourself from your wife's arms.
Give up your sweetest joys!
May the God of Battles not reject you
O brave Canadian boys!

Leave all flowers, gardens and cottages,
Your plough will be at peace in
  your field,
For hark, on all sides of our borders,
Comes the cry for the help of your
  shield. . . . "

Newfoundland

Newfoundland had had a difficult time in the eighteen-sixties. The country was badly polarized during the ferocious election of 1861, which in some constituencies produced pitched battles between Roman Catholics and Protestants. The natural vicissitudes that were to follow during the eighteen-sixties had a numbing effect on sharp political and religious quarrels. Both the inshore and the Banks fishing had been bad since 1860 and were to continue to be so until 1869. The sealing had been poor. Potatoes — a staple in Newfoundland — were badly affected by blight in 1863 and 1864. By 1865, relief of the starving and unemployed took one third of Newfoundland's annual revenue.

Confederation thus came to many in Newfoundland as an outside force strong enough to pull her from the slough she was in. Confederation had a further advantage: it might weaken the old class division between merchant and fisherman, both of whom were caught in the toils of something neither found it easy or possible to throw off. Most merchants appear to have been opposed to Confederation, perhaps for this reason.

Nevertheless, Confederation came as a surprise to Newfoundland. And though some newspapers supported it on the basis of a profound disillusionment with responsible government, the public's instinct was to be cautious. This was reflected in the election of November, 1865. Governor Musgrave, as a result of instructions from London, put great pressure on the Newfoundland government and the Assembly in January, 1866 to declare for Confederation. But even under this kind of pressure all the Assembly would do was to say that although the advantages of Confederation were obvious, great diversity of opinion prevailed about terms. But the Assembly would not consider what terms it would accept.

The election of 1869 was to be decisive. Then the Government did go to the polls on the Confederation issue, and in the first good fishing year for a decade, Confederation was roundly defeated.

72 NO SUPPORT FOR UNION

Patriot, St. John's
Tuesday, November 29, 1864

"We have no faith in a political union with Canada at all. We deem it — 'Better to endure the ills we have, than flee to others that we know not of.'"

73 THE CONFEDERATE BROOM WILL CLEAN UP POLITICAL LIFE

Day Book, St. John's
Wednesday, November 30, 1864

"If the Confederation will cause a thorough sweeping away of this serfdom [especially in the outports], if it shall be the broom which will thoroughly purge this Augean stable — piled up with pauperism, nurtured, forstered, cherished pauperism, — piled up too with a dirty exclusiveness, and yet inhabited by maggots which fatten and flourish upon the decay of more useful animals — then we say by all means let us have the Confederation, or any thing else that will promise relief."

74 NEWFOUNDLAND'S FEARS OF THE BURDENS OF CONFEDERATION

Patriot, St. John's
Tuesday, December 6, 1864

"Nor can we duly comprehend the magnitude of being the contemptible fag-end of such a compact. . . . This Federal scheme is an after-thought of the Canadians. We cannot deny that it is a brilliant thing on paper — this Confederation this Great United British America, which shall reach from 'Newfoundland to the Rocky Mountain[s]' but its brilliancy does not dazzle us as to the duties which must necessarily fall to our share. . . . That TAXATION for all local purposes will be resorted to, is as plain as ABC."

75 THE LOSS OF INDEPENDENCE: A DISADVANTAGE?

Newfoundlander, St. John's
Thursday, January 12, 1865

Letter from C. F. Bennett, dated January 9, 1865. Charles Fox Bennett, a successful merchant and mining promoter, was opposed to Confederation, and his letters are the first guns fired against Confederation, except for the opposition given by the St. John's *Patriot*.

"... I again ask what hope could a youth in this Colony rationally entertain that his interest through the four members of the [future Legislative] Council and the eight members of the General Parliament would have against the political influence which the young men in Canada could exercise in their 195 members, and the youth of the adjoining Provinces over their members, to assure them an appointment to any of those offices?
[Disadvantages of Confederation]:
"The annihilation of our independent Legislature, and of self-legislation, transferring the same to the Canadian Parliament. The power of the Canadian Parliament to tax us without limit.... To vest the power in the Canadian Government to make thereafter all appointments to office in this Colony.
"To give them entire control over our Fisheries, Lands and Minerals. And not least among other calamities, the power to extract the youth, both married and unmarried, of the able-bodied men of the Colony, to shed their blood and leave their bones to bleach in a foreign land, in defence of the Canadian line of boundary and that of the other provinces, and to man also the ships of the Canadian navy."

The *Newfoundlander* replies:
"Mr. Bennett deplores the expected loss of our independent legislation and its transfer to the Canadian Parlia-ment. It is proposed to give the General Government a portion of the powers of legislation we now possess, while we retain for our local Legislature the control of eighty thousand pounds sterling per annum. But what is this 'independent legislation' of which Mr. Bennett is so enamoured? The colony has been going down hill for years past, and what has our independent legislation been able to effect?"

76 MERCANTILE ATTITUDES TO CONFEDERATION

Patriot, St. John's
Saturday, August 12, 1865

This anti-Confederation statement by the St. John's Chamber of Commerce makes clear the stand of the merchants. It was also commented on by Governor Musgrave, in his report to the Colonial Office of August 19, 1865.

"So far as this Chamber is aware, the project of a Confederation of the Provinces was devised as a means of relieving Canada from the political difficulties.... But it is difficult to see what interest this Colony can have in any one of these objects to justify the sacrifice of its independent legislative position, and the assumption of a share of the enormous expenditure that must be incurred for the support of the General Government....
"The Chamber of Commerce is aware of no advantage likely to result from the proposed Confederation, that will at all compensate for these disadvantages.... It can open no new or more extensive market for the products of our fisheries, nor does it hold out a prospect of developing new resources within the Colony, or of extending those we now possess."

77 NEWFOUNDLAND ELECTION OF 1865 AND THE QUESTION OF UNION

Patriot, St. John's
Saturday, September 2, 1865

A Newfoundland general election was called for November, 1865, and it turned out to be about the first election in Newfoundland's history since 1832 in which religion was not a main issue at the polls.

"The paramount question which Voters should take into their consideration between this and the 6th of November next is, not what may be a Candidate's peculiar form of religion . . . but what is his opinion of the contemplated Scheme of Selling Newfoundland to the Canadians? . . . The apparent policy of the Unionists at present is to preserve a death-like silence upon the subject, so as to endeavor to hide the question from the constituencies. If this feint succeeds, the country will be handed over by the Government, without compunction or remorse, to the Canadians, the people will be victimised, but — the CABINET will be permanently provided for at Ottawa!"

78 LOCAL INTERESTS AND FEDERATION: A DIFFERENT VIEW

Courier, St. John's
Saturday, July 14, 1866

The following is a long letter signed "Vindex," dated, Halifax, June 29, 1866, and first published in the Halifax *Evening Express,* a Roman Catholic paper, Wednesday, July 4, 1866. It is quoted at length under the title "Newfoundland and Confederation" by the Newfoundland paper.

" . . . it was impossible for small stores to exist; and now look at the North side of Water Street (the principal Street) and you will find half the houses untenanted. The whole trade of the Country, is in the hands of a dozen merchants, whose object is to bring the Country back to the good old days of the 'fishing Admirals', when only two classes existed — merchants and fishermen. If Confederation were only to break down this grinding monopoly, it would in itself be a blessing.

" . . . As citizens, the merchants are an excellent class — generous to the poor, and ever ready to assist the distressed. In their business capacity they only carry out the old traditional policy handed down from sire to son, which time, like other barbaric relics, will destroy, and the Merchant Princes of Harbor Grace and St. John's, with all their strength and influence, will have to succumb to Confederation."

79 THE NEWFOUNDLAND PRESS AND UNION

Morning Chronicle, St. John's
Saturday, December 22, 1866

The following is an interesting comment on the press and Confederation.

"[The Newfoundland press] have been compelled to scrutinize every question through Government spectacles, and when the Confederation scheme came before them for consideration they argued that because the leaders of the Government were in favor of the measure, their interest lay in adopting it. . . .

"We think, however, that it is not difficult now for the Press to see that the people of this country are not disposed towards Confederation. They have this proof before them — First, that the only paper which opposes Confederation [*i.e.,* the *Morning Chronicle*] is far more extensively read in the country than any other; and second, that it is supported by all classes."

80 A PRO-CONFEDERATE VIEW

Public Ledger, St. John's
Friday, November 30, 1866

The Newfoundland opposition to Confederation is described by a pro-Confederation paper.

"It is understood that a majority of our merchants are strongly opposed to Confederation, and are employing all their influence against the measure. A Minority of them favour the measure; but the bulk of our capitalists are as strongly committed to opposition as ever the landed interest were to the Repeal of the Corn Laws.

"In point of fact, the old relation between merchant and fisherman, has, in the inevitable course of events, already been broken up. No longer, as in the days of yore, does the fisherman, in his simplicity, regard his merchant as a kind of Providence, who will, [sic] exercise a paternal care over him, and feed and cloth [sic] himself and his family, in return for the produce of his toils. A new generation has sprung up who know not the traditions of their fathers; and who look upon the merchant, if not exactly as an enemy, yet as 'fair game'. . . . Now the question arises whether this unhappy, vicious, 'supplying system' can. . . . continue much longer. . . and whether the poverty, idleness, dishonesty it has engendered should not make every lover of his country long for its overthrow?. . . Let confederation come then, and should it slightly increase our taxation, it will make amends by cheapening for us the necessaries of life, giving us free of duty from Canada, breadstuffs, boots, shoes, candles, soap, starch, leather, hard-ware, agricultural implements, manufactures in wood. . . A central Government, with larger vies than any local Legislature could entertain, will initiate improvements and open up our resources. . . . "

Prince Edward Island

It is quite clear from earlier reactions to both the Charlottetown and the Quebec Conferences that Prince Edward Island was not going to join a British North American union unless there were very strong incentives. Happy as she was, complacent, comfortable, and thus callous, Prince Edward Island would not give up her own colonial independence for the sake of four Senators and five M.P.'s in a federal parliament and an Intercolonial Railway that seemed of little immediate value. She wanted more than that, and indeed, in 1873, she was to get it.

Thus the Assembly at Charlottetown administered a decisive defeat to the Quebec Resolutions on March 31, 1865, by a vote of 23-5. The Legislative Council rejected Confederation unanimously. Renewed pressure by the British Government in the summer of 1865 brought a firm and unequivocal answer in 1866, that any federal union "would be opposed to the best and most vital interests" of Prince Edward Island. And that, for the time being, was that.

81 ATTITUDE OF PRINCE EDWARD ISLAND TO FEDERATION

Examiner, Charlottetown
Monday, January 30, 1865

"It is rather singular that mostly all the anti-Unionist controversialists readily admit *Union in the abstract* to be a very good thing. . . . They profess to be very willing to see the field ploughed and harrowed if no crimson-tipped flower would be buried beneath the sod, or no mouse's nest torn and scattered by the unrelenting plough-share. 'Your theory of cultivation,' say they, 'is, for aught we can see to the contrary, sound; but,' they add in tones most melancholy, 'if it be carried into effect, what is to become of the daisies and the mice? Make your system of husbandry consistent with the preservation of daisies and having a due regard for the rights and interests of mice, and the time may, perhaps arrive in which we will give it our favorable consideration.' "

Nova Scotia

There was support for Confederation in Nova Scotia, notably in Halifax, and broadly speaking, along the line of the railway from Halifax to Truro, a line which would become part of the Intercolonial Railway. The Nova Scotia government, under Charles Tupper and his Conservative party, supported Confederation; so did an important section of the Liberal opposition. But here the support ends. The issue weakened the Conservative party, and it split the Liberal party. The Annapolis valley, the south shore, many parts of Cape Breton were broadly opposed. In fact the public generally, in Nova Scotia as in Newfoundland and Prince Edward Island, were more opposed than the politicians. There was a massive debate, on the streets, on public platforms, in the newspapers, and inevitably in the Legislature. There the best Tupper could do, after the defeat of Confederation in New Brunswick in March, 1865, was to produce an innocuous resolution about Maritime union. The real crunch came in the spring of 1866. The Fenian alarms and raid on New Brunswick, together with the turning out of the anti-confederate Smith government in New Brunswick, came in April, 1866; the impetus of these two events allowed Tupper to get a Confederation resolution passed in the Nova Scotia Assembly and in the Legislative Council that very month. After that, despite massive protests, Tupper refused to budge. It is thus important to emphasize that Confederation was passed in Nova Scotia, and with perfect constitutionality. But the means used to pass it were highly dubious; furthermore, the resolute refusal of Tupper to hold an election on the issue made Nova Scotians angry, and after March, 1867, when the British North America Act had passed the British Parliament, bitter and resentful.

82 SUSPICION OF TUPPER'S MOTIVES

Halifax Citizen, Halifax
Saturday, November 5, 1864

" . . . having got power, Tupper intends to keep it at all hazards, and hence he flies to the Confederation scheme. . . . We have very little faith in Confederation as a practical measure; but we have a good deal of faith in Tupper as a political intriguer. Nothing can serve his turn better just now than to divert public attention from Provincial politics. He would annex this Province to Canada, or to Massachusetts, or to the moon, or propose to do so, if by that means he could keep people from talking about his school bill, his retrenchment, his railway duplicity, his tyranny to officials. . . .

"The Liberal leaders, and their organ [the *Morning Chronicle*], have helped him to play his cards, by committing themselves seriously, as they appear to have done, to the Confederacy. As matters now stand he has the game entirely in his own hands. The opposition have not the power either to carry or defeat the Confederation scheme. . . . "

83 THE ISSUES INVOLVED AS SEEN BY A NOVA SCOTIAN NEWSPAPER

Yarmouth Herald, Yarmouth
Thursday, November 17, 1864

"Several of the leading journals of all the Provinces have come out strongly in opposition to the measure [Confederation], and we trust that the people will earnestly consider the question before it be too late. The tariff of Canada is at least 50 per cent higher than that of this Province, and as the country is largely involved in debt and has important public works in prospect, the duties on importations are likely to be still further increased. Are the people of this Province willing to have their taxes raised, probably doubled, and the revenue appropriated to a Federal Legislature in which they will have little voice, and in which they will be entirely at the mercy of Canada? . . . Are they, then, prepared to be taxed so much, to risk so much, to surrender their Legislative independence merely for the purpose of inducing Canada to become a partner in a road [the Intercolonial railway] which is of infinitely more importance to her than to them?"

84 FEDERATION AND THE QUESTION OF THE FRONTIER

Morning Chronicle, Halifax
Saturday, November 19, 1864

"So far as we have been able to sound public opinion, the project of a legislative union of the Provinces of Nova Scotia, New Brunswick, and P. E. Island was popular in Nova Scotia . . . . However, there was not a chance for it at Charlottetown. It was therefore no question of choice on the part of the Delegates from this Province, whether they preferred a Legislative Union of the Maritime Provinces or a Federal Union of the whole, the only election left was, whether they would, or would not entertain a project for the Federation of British America. . . .

"But why any change, it will be said, Why not let well enough alone? But we are quite sure that well enough would let us alone? . . . With a thousand miles of frontier in a state of angry excitement. . . . "

85 DISSATISFACTION OVER THE LIMITATIONS OF THE CONFEDERATION SCHEME

Halifax Citizen, Halifax
Saturday, November 19, 1864

"It will be hard work to excite enthusiasm for the Confederation scheme which our provincial politicians concocted at Quebec. . . . Even those who most earnestly advocated British American Union receive with marked disappointment the announcement of a project which falls very far short of what their aspirations induced them to expect.

"We frankly avow that this is our feeling. . . . In fact, as a Union measure, the Confederation scheme is impracticable; its inevitable effect would be, instead of abolishing, to intensify sectionalism by bringing sectional interests not into combination but into collision . . . It makes no matter that it [the Confederation scheme] has given these local legislatures very little to do. The Legislatures have to meet, and having met, they will find something to do, if they have to make employment — to elaborate grievances or increase taxes. . . . a sectional legislature under a general congress is only a nursery of sectional feeling, a fruitful factory for local jealousies, grievances and deadlocks to progress."

86 THE OPPONENTS OF CONFEDERATION

Evening Reporter, Halifax
Saturday, December 10, 1864

"Our capitalists are in the front rank of opposition. These are so because an union will disturb their present arrangements and modify considerably their future plans. Another reason for their opposition is because they see that the influx of further capital will influence the state of the money market, and will increase their difficulty in investing. . . . Many of our merchants are strenuous opponents of union because union in their estimation means more business men, greater competition, less profits, more trouble. . . . Our dry goods men are opposed to an union because they fear that for them union means fifteen or twenty per cent *ad valorem* duty. . . . ."

87 THE FINANCIAL ASPECT OF UNION

Bullfrog, Halifax
Saturday, December 17, 1864

"Dreams of a United British North America may be very cheering and we hope some day to see the great Union effected, but such dreams can afford no excuse to our politicians for concealing the disadvantages and arguing the benefits of the scheme. . . . Their business is with the present [,] and a sensible population is not prone to dreaming. . . .

"The financial portion of the Confederation scheme is its most important feature. Since no real union is in contemplation, but rather a careful bargain between Canada and the Lower Provinces — free trade and an Intercolonial line offered by the former, and a Union which will loose Canada's political deadlock by the latter — the fiscal portion of the agreement assumes a gigantic importance."

88 A PLEA FOR THE END OF LOCALISM

Unionist and Halifax Journal, Halifax
Monday, January 23, 1865

" . . . in the General Parliament and Central Government under this Union, we hope and believe that Nova Scotia, like each and every one of the other Colonies comprised in it, will be effectually swamped; that we shall then hear nothing of any local parties; that then our public men will not be known as Canadians, and New Brunswickers, and Nova Scotians, but only as British Americans. That, we hold to be one of the leading objects which the Union has in view. In the Central Government and Parliament, it must be that what is seen to be the interest of one section of the Confederation must be the interest of all."

89 CONFEDERATION: FEAR OF WHAT IT COULD INVOLVE

Morning Chronicle, Halifax
Monday, January 30, 1865

Letter to the editor from "A Conservative Liberal" states a familiar attitude in Nova Scotia. The *Morning Chronicle* had now gone over to the anti-confederate side.

"Federation is the dragon's teeth, sown in British North America, for we forsee that they will start up into armed men, whenever a stone shall be thrown by some unwary hand. It matters little whence the stone may come; it will be certain to fall in the chapter of future events. Some Local Legislature, that considers its reserved rights to have been trampled upon will declare its paramount authority to have been trifled with. . . . What on earth are we to gain by putting our heads under this great extinguishing fool's-cap of a Confederation? Is it a government of twenty-one branches that we admire?"

90 PROVINCIALISM: THE PATH TO SUCCESS

Morning Chronicle, Halifax
Wednesday, February 8, 1865

The following is a part of Howe's "Brotheration Letter No. 10". For other quotations see J. Murray Beck, *Joseph Howe: The Voice of Nova Scotia* (Toronto: McClelland and Stewart, 1964).

"We [in Nova Scotia] have a low tariff, an overflowing treasury, and own more tonnage [of ships] than any 350,000 people on the face of the globe. . . . Here are lines of 'progress' distinctly marked, that we may advance upon without peril or impediment; with no distant authority to control us — with no outward drain upon our public and private resources; and we say in all sincerity to our people, let us work out our destiny upon these lines, without running away, above tide-water, after the will-of-the-wisp at Ottawa, which will land us in a Slough of Despond."

91 IMMEDIATE UNION

British Colonist, Halifax
Thursday, February 28, 1865

Of all the rhodomontade urging Confederation in Nova Scotia, one editorial deserves remark for its cogency and realism. It can be added that a week after this, the defeat of Tilley in the New Brunswick elections put out of court, for the time being, discussion of Confederation in the Nova Scotian Assembly.

"Union is immediately necessary on account of commercial causes. Our present position is without parallel in the history of the world. The Italian peninsula, before the recent consolidation, bore the nearest resemblance to it. It was composed of a number of petty states, each with its own laws and institutions, its own jealously guarded frontiers, and everlasting Dogana [Customs]. So we here in all the British American Provinces meet with the everlasting Custom House. It is a disgrace to the British Empire that Nova Scotia should levy duties on the manufactures of New Brunswick. Yet nothing can pass between these two Provinces without being entered at Customs. On the surface even [,] such a system is bad enough; but there are evils connected with it which reach far down beneath the surface, and affect all trade and commerce. . . .

"Union is immediately necessary so as to abolish all differences in currency, and in trade regulations. Each little Province has now its own Government, and even its own postage stamp. Prince Edward Island has one system of currency; Nova Scotia another; New Brunswick another; Newfoundland a fourth; and Canada a fifth. Here is endless confusion and a fruitful source of local jealousy, of sectional alienation, and narrow provincialism. But its most direct and positive effect is felt in trade; since all that tends to interfere with financial operations will produce evil effects in the general commerce of a country. The day then that shall abolish all these miserable local coinages, currencies, and postage-stamps, cannot dawn too soon.

"We want Union immediately, for the sake of the Intercolonial Railroad. Our country is British America. But as yet the most important parts are kept asunder by a wilderness. . . .

"Union is immediately necessary for political reasons. The Nova Scotian now is without a country. He cannot call himself an American. He is not an Englishman. As a Nova Scotian, he is nothing; for it is only the district of a district. The highest political prize in his native province is at best but a small one. His real country, however, is here, only he cannot yet claim it. It spreads over the continent; but it is divided and subdivided by many barriers into many States. . . .

"There is not a circumstance in our position, or prospects, or hopes, or fears, which does not demand Union, immediate, instant Union. It should have been done before; but since it was not, let it at least be effected now. Our sympathies, our feelings, our interests, all draw us together. The Providence that watches over nations has given us this golden opportunity. Let it be the determination of every Nova Scotian to seize the opportunity for — 'Now is the accepted time!' "

Cape Breton — and we imagine there would be a great deal — there would be a rush, not merely 'across the [New Brunswick] border', but all the way to the head of Lake Ontario, away out to the Hudson's Bay Territory. The laborers might not like to go so far from home, but then they would be reconciled if they saw that the great statesmen who had brought about this grand scheme of Confederation were 'reaping the rich reward' of their 'foresight' in that magnificent structure at Ottawa, which counts its plaister by acres and its cornices by miles."

---

92 THE FUTURE OF NOVA SCOTIA UNDER CONFEDERATION

Morning Chronicle, Halifax
Tuesday, December 12, 1865

A projection of what would happen to Nova Scotia under Confederation by an anti-Confederate paper.

"We would [under Confederation], it is true have our 80 cents a head, amounting to $264,000 a year, equal to our annual road grant. That is all we would get back in exchange for over a million of dollars under a 10 per cent. ad valorem tariff — that's all we would get back under a 20 per cent. Canadian tariff, even if it realized two millions a year. All the surplus would go — where? To purchase the Hudson Bay Territory — to build the Georgian Bay Canal — to enlarge the canals already built — to open up the North West territory, and build fortifications. Anywhere, everywhere, but in the little Province of Nova Scotia, with its 19 representatives in a House of 194 members. There would then be no more railways built in Nova Scotia by Government funds. . . . Everywhere our public works would be brought to a dead lock. And if there should then be 'surplus labor' in Nova Scotia and

93 HOWE'S SPEECH AT WINDSOR, NOVA SCOTIA

Morning Chronicle, Halifax
Saturday, May 19, 1866

Howe here complains of continuous misrepresentation of his past speeches by pro-Confederation newspapers.

"Every old speech that I had ever made in favor of the Intercolonial railroad — every pretty picture I had drawn of the scenery or resources of Canada — every illustration with which I had enlivened national questions or other people's proposals for union of any kind, were raked up and perverted till thousands were mystified and nobody knew what to believe."

The sign over the door to this meeting had the following:
"Land of the Mayflower, home of the free
Don't sell your country to Darcy McGee."

94 THOUGHTS ON CONFEDERATION

Yarmouth Tribune, Yarmouth
Wednesday, June 27, 1866

"We of the Maritime Provinces are required to give up, not only those inestimable privileges of self-government won nearly thirty years since from the officials of Downing Street, but rights and powers of which we have enjoyed for more than a century. . . . The loss of self-control will be as total and complete as the loss of revenue. The laws which affect our most intimate social and business relations with our fellow-men, will in the event of Union, instead of being as now enacted by a body identified with us in every possible way — will depend upon the fiat of a motely assemblage of men from various scattered and dissimilar provinces, the majority of whom will be absolutely beyond our control, and whom the public opinion of our people cannot in the slightest degree affect."

New Brunswick

New Brunswick has the most complicated story of any of the Atlantic colonies. To begin with, political parties in New Brunswick were not parties really; rather, they were diverse groups thrown up by the apposition of political groups in the familiar two-sided Assembly of British colonies, the apposition, in other words, of the ins and the outs. It is fair to say that all British North American political parties had something of this looseness; in New Brunswick, for reasons embedded in the character and traditions of New Brunswick history, these tendencies were rampant. The issues that divided politics in New Brunswick were, thus, more apt to be patronage and railways than Liberal and Conservative. The Tilley government, elected in 1862, was nominally Liberal; the opposition was a collection of ex-Liberals and quondam Conservatives.

So in New Brunswick Confederation was a complication of all other existing political issues. New Brunswickers were closer to Canada, and, also, to the United States, and they had a sharper appreciation of the advantages of union than did the other Atlantic provinces. This appreciation was, however, given the context of New Brunswick history, heavily on the material benefits of Confederation. This was mainly on the prospects for an Intercolonial railway. On the other side, against Confederation, was a fear, widely shared in the other Atlantic colonies, of the higher Canadian tariff.

Leonard Tilley took Confederation to the people of New Brunswick in March, 1865, in a general election. Whether his timing was right has been much debated, and there is some evidence that Lieutenant-Governor Arthur Gordon forced Tilley's hand. An election was in any case due within a year; the question was one of timing. In any event, the result was a disaster, both to the immediate prospects of Confederation in New Brunswick, and more important, to its prospects in Nova Scotia and in the Province of Canada. Tilley was personally defeated and his government shattered. His followers were reduced to a group of 11 in a 41-seat Assembly. Many defeats were, however, on fairly narrow majorities, some so narrow that the new Premier, A. J. Smith, felt it impossible to open certain constitutencies by making cabinet appointments. This in turn helps to explain the events of 1866.

The Albert Smith government was

composed of diverse elements with a variety of interests. Pressure from the British Government in the summer of 1865 may have strengthened the determination of several members of that government to stick to their opposition to Confederation, but at the same time it forced other members of it to reconsider their opposition to Confederation. More important, it seems to have weakened the government's strength in the province as a whole.

In the spring of 1866 the climax came. The Smith government was attacked from two sides: strong pressure from the Lieutenant-Governor, Arthur Gordon, to declare for a Confederation policy of some kind, and an opposition determined to bring them down if possible. The pressure from the British Government had taken the form of emphasizing the necessity of Confederation for purposes of defence; thus the Fenian crisis of March and April, 1866, was made to order for those who wanted to bring the Smth government to ruin. It was in circumstances of this kind, that Arthur Gordon was able to force the resignation of the Smith government, on April 10, 1866.

A new government that supported Confederation was now called into existence, led by Peter Mitchell and Leonard Tilley. An election was thus necessary, and an election was held in May, 1866. This election restored the Confederates to control in the Assembly. Smith was defeated, even more decisively than Tilley had been the year before. The rest was inevitable.

95 CONFEDERATION AND LOCAL LEGISLATURES: THE CONTINUATION OF A BAD SYSTEM

Daily Evening Globe, Saint John
Monday, October 17, 1864

"One of the worst features of the Union plan proposed by Canada is, that it will leave our local legislatures still in existence. It is true, that it is proposed to shear them of many of their privileges. . . . [but, nevertheless] each Province will become a large commonalty. . . . Conceive, if you can, the style of men that will offer themselves for seats in the local legislature. — Things are bad enough now . . . pettifogging politicians, whose statesmanship will consist in engineering situations for themselves and their friends, and whose patriotism will be developed in filling their own pockets at the expense of the State . . . . While the local legislatures will be principally composed of men of this class . . . they will at the same time have immense power. . . . A Legislative Union of the Colonies would have swept local bodies away altogether, and this could have been done with great advantage to the public welfare."

96 WILL CONFEDERATION MAKE THE LOCAL LEGISLATURES REDUNDANT?

Morning Freeman, Saint John
Thursday, November 3, 1864

" . . . the bodies called local Legislatures [in the Quebec scheme] will be merely central municipalities, with less power than the St. John Common Council now has. It is absurd to speak of such a Union as is thus describad [*sic*] as a Confederation. It is in truth a Legislative Union, and the local Legislatures will be useless, cumbrous, expensive machinery, which no one will desire to see retained. Their very first session will prove them worthless, and when they have served the purpose of deluding some of the people by a show of Federal Union, they will be abolished. If this Union must be, it would be better to abolish the local Legislatures at once in appearances as well as reality than to set up such expensive shams."

97 THE CASE FOR LOCAL LEGISLATURES WITHIN THE FEDERAL SYSTEM

New Brunswick Reporter, Fredericton Friday, November 25, 1864

Charles Fisher, one of the New Brunswick delegates to both the Charlottetown and Quebec Conferences, gave this speech at Woodstock, New Brunswick on his return from Quebec.

"There are many who say they prefer a Legislative Union [of British North America], so do I, and although this proposed union is called a Federation, it really goes far beyond that, and is in all the essential requisites a Legislative union. Aware of the difficulties [however] which would surround the attempt in one general and central Legislature like that of England, to regulate and control the local affairs of the separate portions of the Confederation, it is provided that large powers shall be vested in the local Legislatures [,] enabling the people thus to have immediate control of their purely local affairs, reserving to the different Provinces certain interests and rights peculiar to themselves, and over which the general Parliament has no constitutional power to Legislate.

" . . . We desired to lay the foundations of a good government with a strong and vigorous executive. . . . In adopting the British Constitution as a model, we knew that where it has been established it had secured as great an amount of political liberty as the people required; that though it was the growth of ages, such was its elasticity, it had adapted itself to every age, to every country, to every condition of things. . . . "

98 IMAGINATION: THE MISSING LINK IN NEW BRUNSWICK'S RESPONSE TO FEDERATION?

Daily Evening Globe, Saint John Monday, December 5, 1864

" . . . for years past our local politics have turned almost wholly upon some question of taxation. . . . It is not, then, singular that New Brunswick is the only Province in which the question of the cost of Confederation is the main point for discussion. Instead of Mr. Tilley coming before the people and urging them to accept Confederation because of its many benefits, and to dwell grandly upon what it is to do for us, he is compelled to resort to various plans to prove that we ought to accept it, because it is not going to cost us any more than we pay now. Neither in Canada or in Nova Scotia, so far, does the financial part of the scheme seem to be considered of the first importance. Even this journal is compelled to yield to the force of public opinion and to ask for explanations about financial trifles. . . . If increased taxation will make us a great people; if it will settle our lands; if it will open our mines; if it will build our railroads; . . . if it will make us a great nation . . . if it will make us the centre of civilization to which the down trodden and oppressed of other lands will come for succor and shelter, then, [i]ndeed, we will do well to take it, and Confederation together.

"That our people are not satisfied with our present position and status can not be denied. There are in our hearts thousands of unsatisfied longings and of deep aspirations urging us towards nationality. These may be vain; but they exist; they may be checked for a time; but they cannot be repressed entirely. They may originate only in our imagination, and the imagination of a young people is wild and exuberant as that of youth itself — but imagination governs the world (according to Napoleon) and it is a much more powerful agent for the promoters of the Confederation scheme to operate upon than all the columns of figures they have yet arrayed in support of their project."

99 FEDERATION IN CANADA AND THE MARITIMES: DIFFERENCE OF APPROACH NEEDED

Head Quarters, Fredericton
Wednesday, December 7, 1864

On Galt's Sherbrooke speech, of November 23.

"The Canadian delegates, in pressing the scheme upon the [Canadian] people, stand on vantage ground compared with their brethren from the Lower Provinces. They have a pressing difficulty to overcome which they must at once meet; they must provide some immediate remedy for their grave political difficulties; the people are prepared for some measure to meet the crisis, and it is not so difficult a task to make the scheme acceptable to them as it is to the people of the Lower Provinces, upon whom it has come unexpectedly, and who will resist it strongly if they think there will be an attempt made to force it upon them."

100 ANGER AT BRITISH IGNORANCE OF BRITISH NORTH AMERICA

Weekly Telegraph, Saint John
Wednesday, January 11, 1865

British North Americans often complained that the British newspapers knew little or nothing about British possessions in North America, and what little they did know was inaccurate and prejudiced.

Whatever else be the result of Confederation, Great Britain "will learn that the now fragmentary and disunited elements of the 'Colonial Empire' are not mere lumbering camps and the semi-civilized homes of a rude and uneducated people, but possess the wealth and enterprise necessary for a nation. . . . [British newspapers] show more knowledge of Kamchatka . . . than they do of British North America, and particularly the Maritime provinces. . . . One does not mind the besotted New York *Herald* speaking of the Lower Provinces as 'fishing villages', it is part of its low buffoonery to do so; but we should like to see a Press, whose good opinion is worth the having, but who are really ignorant of us, placed in . . . " [the rest of this is missing.]

101 THE POWER OF THE LOCAL VOICE IN A FEDERAL UNION

Colonial Farmer, Fredericton
Monday, January 16, 1865

Report of a speech of Leonard Tilley at the Fredericton Temperance Hall, on January 5.

Maritime union, Tilley said, had made property values in Fredericton all uncertain, because the capital of a united "Acadia" would certainly not be Fredericton. In the case of Confederation, however, the position would be very different. "Why, the seat of the local Government . . . would be secured forever. But some may object to this the Legislative business would be so much reduced, and there would be such a consequent reduction of expenditure of public money, that it would be hardly worth keeping. Now, he (Mr. Tilley) would reply to this, that he had taken the trouble to examine, and he found there were but seven Bills out of all that were passed last Winter that would not still be subjects of local legislation. . . .

"Upon this [the question of disallowance] Mr. Tilley very properly observed, that we had experienced no inconvenience, and no complaints had been heard nothwithstanding all our laws hitherto were subject to the approval of the Queen in Council. Her Majesty being always guided in such cases by the advice of the Colonial Secretary. Now how does the case stand? As we are, every act of every kind, is subject to veto, by a power, in whose councils we have no voice, much less a vote, while in the case of Federation, we should have 15 Representatives in the House of Commons, 10 in the Legislative Council; and would, no doubt, have at least one, perhaps more, in the Executive."

102 A CYNICAL VIEW OF HOW CONFEDERATION WAS ACHIEVED

Borderer, Sackville
Friday, January 27, 1865

A. J. Smith was to become Premier of New Brunswick after the provincial election of March, 1865. This amusing speech suggests a number of points around which Maritime opposition gathered.

" . . . a delegation of the clever men from Canada came down [to Charlottetown.] All this time the matter [of Confederation] had never been before the people. Did they ever hear of it? He had never heard of it! In three days the Canadian delegates had con-verted the others. What inducements were held out, what nice times they would have by and bye, when the Government offices were distributed. Their delegates threw themselves entirely into the hands of the Canadians, their judgement was lost — they had great dinners by day and great balls by night — they came home reporting that a union of the maritime provinces was impracticable . . . They went [up to Quebec] taking with them several ladies who they knew are always in favor of union. They had nice times going up and nicer after they got there; all they did was in secret, confidential, was the like ever done before, 'twas passing strange. Mr. Palmer [of Prince Edward Island] tells that they did not think alike . . . at last a happy idea struck some one — it was suggested as a first principle, that the governors of the different Provinces should be appointed by the General Government — this worked liked a charm, all was harmony, all things went well after this, it was a happy family . . . Nova Scotia sent Tupper and McCully, in affectionate embrace, and Archibald and Dickey in blissful ignorance of political warfare — from New Brunswick they had the smiling, rosy-cheeked leader of the Government [Tilley] tickling the venerable ex-premier, Chandler, with a Governor's commission and P. E. Island too, exhibited the lion and the lamb lying down together. (Here the cheering and roars of laughter drowned the voice of the speaker.) They had a fat time, dinners, balls, champaign [sic], suppers, and when surrounded with such influences were they fit to form a new empire. After setting sixteen days this wonderful creature [Confederation] made its appearance. . . . "

103 BELIEF THAT A FEDERAL UNION WILL LEAD TO A LEGISLATIVE UNION

Weekly Telegraph, Saint John
Wednesday, February 1, 1865

" . . . we feel satisfied that the Federal Union will in a few years be changed into a Legislative Union. If we thought otherwise we would not write a line in its defence. If we were convinced that the double expense of maintaining a General Legislature as well as some half dozen Local Legislatures is to be perpetuated; if we were satisfied that the twopenny-ha'penny Parliaments which may for some years to come be convened at Fredericton, Halifax and Charlottetown, were to be maintained and fastened on the finances of the respective Provinces, we would oppose the Scheme to the bitter end.

"We do trust, therefore, that as we proceed in the discussion of this important question, and try conscientiously to discover what the real fruits of Confederation shall be, we shall hear no more of this paltry hobby of taxation. It is a matter of minor moment."

104 VOX POPULI. . . . .

Standard, St. Andrews
Wednesday, February 8, 1865

"*Confederation* meetings are being held all over the Province, Charlotte County fully alive on the great question, has set the ball in motion by the Meetings held at St. Stephen last week. . . . [Supporters or opponents] should submit gracefully to the decision of the people, who themselves are crying for light, that they may decide discreetly. They feel that a great crisis is upon them — that the question of a Confederation of the Colonies, should not be hastily rejected — and that all the information in possession of our statesmen should be given. Nothing but fear of 'taxation' will prevent many from voting for it; this obstacle once removed will pave the way for its adoption."

105 THE CHOICES BEFORE THE PROVINCES

Morning Journal, Saint John
Wednesday, October 11, 1865

"It seems to us that the British North American Provinces must either accept the Quebec Scheme, modify it, or by remaining as they are, isolated, and antagonistic as respect to each other. . . . soon drift separately, or together, into a Union with the United States."

106 EFFECT OF THE FENIAN MANIFESTO ON CONFEDERATION

Charlotte Advocate, St. Stephen, as quoted by the New Brunswick Reporter, Fredericton
Friday, April 27, 1866

The Fenian raid at Indian Island in the St. Croix estuary, Saturday, April 14, 1866, seriously weakened the cause of the New Brunswick anti-Confederates.

"It was an unlucky hour for the anti-Confederates when Mr. Killian [the leader of the Fenians] put forth his manifesto declaring against Confederation. Nothing could have been done equal to it to carry Confederation. Those who opposed the Scheme and who yet dislike it will sink that and many other objectionable points, in their love for British institutions, and allegiance to the British Flag."

C. 1867

On March 29, 1867, the Queen gave royal approval to the British North America Act. It was now law, and there remained only to proclaim July 1, 1867 as the date of its implementation.

On March 30, 1867, W. H. Seward, the American Secretary of State, and the Russian Minister to Washington, signed the agreement for the American purchase of Alaska for $7 million. The purchase was ratified by the United States Senate by an overwhelming vote, 37 to 2, and proclaimed by President Andrew Johnson on June 20, 1867.

The connection between the American acquisition of Alaska and British North American Confederation was not entirely accidental. Charles Sumner urged ratification of the Alaska purchase on the ground that it was a "visible step in the occupation of the whole North American continent." This may have been bombast; but there were similar remarks in New York newspapers, British newspapers, as well as in British dispatches from Washington to London: that is, the reason for the American acquisition was not the intrinsic value of Alaska (whatever that was) but the hope of acquiring the territory that lay between Alaska and the 49th parallel.

All of this was felt by British North Americans, and on the west coast it was felt more sharply. British Columbians cared little enough about Alaska itself; but they cared very much about the kind of moral and physical energy displayed by the government that had bought it. It contrasted unpleasantly with what appeared to be the supineness of the British Government.

Until 1866 British Columbia and Vancouver Island were two separate British colonies. British Columbia had been made a Crown colony in 1858; Vancouver Island had been first a proprietary colony of the Hudson's Bay Company, and after 1859 a Crown colony. The Fraser gold rush of 1858 had contributed to both of those changes, and it had made each colony superficially prosperous. When the gold strike petered out by 1865, the prosperity of both colonies collapsed. They were joined together in a union, called British Columbia, at the end of 1866.

The year 1867, was then, for British Columbians a year of yearning — for a change in their political and their economic fortunes. Would annexation be the answer? There was talk of annexation. Union with the United States seemed a closer, a more realistic, possibility than any union with the distant east of British North America. Moreover, annexation did not carry, not on the west coast, the same overtones of disloyalty that it did in the east. Nevertheless, however disgusted British Columbians may have been with the sleepy British lion, there was a genuine sense of belonging to the British colonial family. The Confederation movement in these circumstances is not altogether surprising; what is surprising is that it was as strong as it was.

In the old Province of Canada, Confederation came in with a good deal of enthusiasm. Ontario was now free to enjoy its own local government, and within a federal system, its longed-for "rep. by pop."; Quebec got its own provincial government and its provincial capital at old Quebec city; and at Ottawa the new central government of the Dominion began the administration of its enormous and growing domain. There was, however, some heartburning in Nova Scotia over the loss of its old independence and a disposition in New Brunswick, within Confederation, and in Prince Edward Island and Newfoundland, outside of it, to see how things went. There were difficulties, both in New Brunswick and Nova Scotia, between 1867 and 1869, but by 1870, the better terms of 1869 and the prosperity of 1869 and 1870 were already starting to dissolve older loyalties, and to suggest the first glimmers of a new one.

Vancouver Island and British Columbia

107 SUPPORT FOR NORTH AMERICAN FEDERATION

Weekly British Colonist, Victoria
Tuesday, August 16, 1864

The editor of this paper was an émigré Nova Scotian, Amor de Cosmos, né William Smith, who arrived in Victoria via California. His enthusiasm was not always matched by good sense; still, his editorial here says something of the frustrations of the colonial condition that urged so many toward Confederation.

"With the ordinary course of Canadian politics, the interests of neither Vancouver Island or British Columbia are closely interwoven; but the recent mail has brought us intelligence of a movement. . . . which, if carried into effect, is likely in the course of time to bring the Colonies of the Pacific within the political folds of a great North American constitution. . . . We hail this first movement of the Canadian Government as the commencement of the regeneration of the hitherto apron-stringed colonists. With a federation of colonies from one ocean to the other, what limits can be placed to our material greatness, and what to our political aspirations? Instead of colonial talent being 'cabined, cribbed, confined,' to the barren area of local politics, its horizon will be extended across a continent. . . . we can only hope that the movement may be thoroughly successful, and thus enable us at no distant date, to emerge from our helplessness and isolation. . . . "

108 CONFEDERATION IS DEFEATED IN NEW BRUNSWICK

Victoria Weekly Chronicle, Victoria
Tuesday, May 2, 1865

"From the information before us, we should say that they [the supporters of Confederation] will not have long to wait. With such an army of allies as the Federation party had in the contest in New Brunswick, defeated as the scheme was by such a small majority and by such rotten make-believes . . . [the victory of Confederation seems certain. Union has to come;] the young colonists go across the lines and in a few months return with [American] naturalization papers, and something more. . . . The literature of Boston and New York is on every shelf, the tools and implements of Connecticut, on every farm and in every workshop and the politics of Washington on every tongue. Perhaps these things are not Americanizing the British Colonies and paving the way for annexation, but we are not so sure of it. Give the colonist a country and a nation of which to be proud and you prevent it."

109 CONFEDERATION: THE NEED FOR BALANCED JUDGEMENT

British Columbian, New Westminster
Saturday, June 1, 1867

This is a comment by a sober John Robson (from Perth, Canada West), on one of the more ebullient editorials of de Cosmos in the Victoria *Colonist* on Confederation.

"To rant about the utter ruin of our magnificent colony and roar for immediate admission into the new Dominion, as the only means of saving us from 'annexation' or something worse, is, in our humble opinion, simply to prejudice our cause. . . . It is both impolitic and untrue. . . . We must not 'throw ourselves away' while smarting under the effects of a temporary depression."

Alaska Purchase by the United States

110 THE EFFECTS OF THE UNITED STATES' PURCHASE OF ALASKA

Morning Telegraph, Saint John
Tuesday, April 2, 1867

"Why British diplomatists did not step in and secure the region [Alaska] is a mystery. The effect of allowing the United States to occupy territory north, as well as south, of British possessions, will be to give rise to . . . probably fresh aggressions on the part of the States. . . . the acquisition of territory on our northwestern frontier by the ever-grasping Republic, although producing momentary dissatisfaction among Colonists, may turn out to be a blessing, since it cannot fail to arouse in the breasts of Imperial statesmen a sense of danger — a danger that can only be averted by immediate attention to the proper means of communication with their sister Provinces on the Atlantic seaboard, together with a proper system of settlement, which will cause the stream of settlement to flow to the British possessions of the North-West."

111 UNITED STATES PHOBIA

Quebec Daily Mercury, Quebec
Saturday, May 25, 1867

Report of Galt's speech at Lennoxville of Thursday, May 23.

"If the United States desire to outflank us on the West [by the acquisition of Alaska], we must accept the situation, and lay our hand on British Columbia and the Pacific Ocean. This country cannot be surrounded by the United States — we are gone if we allow it. . . . We must have our back to the North."

---

112 A WEST COAST VIEW OF THE PURCHASE

British Columbian, New Westminster
Wednesday, July 3, 1867

" . . . Americans have been mulcted in seven millions [of dollars] for the doubtful luxury of an Arctic preserve in which to cool the ardour of their 'manifest destiny' aspirations. . . . "

An End and a Beginning

113 RESOLUTION AT FORT GARRY

Nor'Wester, Winnipeg
Saturday, December 29, 1866

A Report of a Public Meeting held at Fort Garry in mid-December. The following resolution, among others, was passed. The resolution here is important in the light of the complete failure of the Dominion Government in 1868 and 1869 to consider the wishes of the Red River people. The report of this meeting is also quoted in the New Westminster *British Columbian*, February 27, 1867.

"That in consequence of the great political changes which the British North American Provinces are now on the eve of undergoing, and the settlement of the Hudson's Bay question, that no further delay should take place in creating the Red River a Crown colony, with the view of joining Confederation under conditions which may be submitted for the approval of the people. . . . "

114 ROLE OF THE LIBERAL PARTY IN CONFEDERATION

Le Pays, Montreal
Tuesday, June 4, 1867 [translation]

"The confederation exists in name only for the power of the local governments is so limited and so subordinated to the control of the alleged federal government, that no prestige of sovereignty remains to the governments of the individual provinces. . . .

"In all this there are many reasons for clashes between the local and federal authorities . . . and when these questions arise the Liberal Party will fulfill its duty in supporting any measure which will decentralise power and give the widest freedom of action to local authority. . . .

"In a word, in the interests of Lower Canada, the Liberal Party will have to seek to impart new elasticity to the federal link and reject centralising elements in the distribution of powers . . . . "

115 DISTRUST OF POLITICIANS

Morning Chronicle, Halifax
Monday, June 3, 1867

"Nothing in our past condition demanded this movement. This Province, and the other Provinces in a less marked degree, were prosperous: there was no cry for change heard from the people; they were content with their condition. But the politicians of Canada wanted some change to enable them to escape their continual deadlocks; and the politicians of this and adjoining Province of New Brunswick, anxious for a wider field upon which to display themselves, and for larger salaries than their prudent constituents would allow them to take, were only too ready to lend themselves to any scheme, no matter how wild, provided it offered a chance of securing the objects of their ambition. . . . "

116 THE DEATH OF THE COLONIAL LEGISLATURE OF NEW BRUNSWICK

Morning Freeman, Saint John
Saturday, June 15, 1867

A satirical obituary on the last session of the colonial legislature of New Brunswick.

"Died — At her late residence, in the City of Fredericton the 20th May last, from the effects of an accident which she received in April, 1866 [the dismissal of the Smith ministry], and which she bore with a patient resignation to the will of Providence [Great Britain], the Province of New Brunswick, in the 83rd year of her age. The deceased was attended during her last illness, by Dr. [A. J.] Smith, who did all that mortal man could do to prolong her life, and he thinks he would have been successful but for a bitter dose a quack gave her, who used to deal in pills [Leonard Tilley, a druggist in Saint John]; this brought on a relapse from which it was impossible to relieve her. The body will lie in State till the first day of July, 1867, when the funeral will take place from her late residence to the grave yard at Ottawa. . . .

"On the day of the funeral business of all kinds will be suspended, the stores are to be closed and flags hung at half mast. All true sons of New Brunswick are requested to go in mourning for their poor lost mother, and to offer up their prayers for the repose of her soul in the next world of darkness and uncertainty."

117 TIME AND CONFEDERATION

Sarnia Observer, Sarnia
Friday, June 28, 1867

"Had it been known, in June, 1864, that it would take three years to make Confederation the law of the land, the Reform party could not possibly have been brought to accept it. . . . Reference to the newspaper articles, the speeches in Parliament, and the speeches made out of Parliament, by members, after their return home [end of June, 1864], will show that in 1864 the universal expectation of the country was that the Federation, either of all the Provinces together, or of the two Canadas together. . . would be carried in about a year from June, 1864; cer-

tainly before the year 1866 should have closed."

118 THOUGHTS ON CONFEDERATION

Examiner, Charlottetown
Monday, June 17, 1867

"As the majority of the people on this Island are still determined to shut their eyes to whatever advantages Confederation may possess, it would be useless to write anything on the subject at present. If we disparaged the grand project, we might get a large audience; but we prefer to wait in order to see how it works in the other provinces."

Examiner, Charlottetown
Monday, July 1, 1867

"Here, alas! the great public of Prince Edward Island treat the thing [Confederation] with feelings akin to contempt."

119 GOOD-WILL AND RESERVATION TOWARD CONFEDERATION

Progress, Summerside
Monday, July 1, 1867

"Today witnesses the birth of the New Dominion, and we do not doubt but that all good Confederates here as well as in the Dominion itself will experience a new sensation — will feel a spark of genuine patriotism kindling in their bosoms.

"However, the Dominion is launched upon the sea of history; and though we do not admire the build of the craft, we cannot fail in our heart to wish her other than a prosperous voyage. All we ask for is our Island to be let alone, until we see how the

Dominion works. We fear there is shipwreck ahead. In fact breakers are already to be seen surrounding the Nova Scotia coast. . . . We believe in destiny; but we do not consider the destiny of the Dominion sufficiently manifest as yet."

120 A NEW AGE IS BORN

Globe, Toronto
Monday, July 1, 1867

"With the first dawn of this gladsome midsummer morn, we hail this birthday of a new nationality. A united British America, with its four millions of people, takes its place this day among the nations of the world . . . . Old things have passed away. The history of old Canada, with its contracted bounds, and limited divisions of Upper and Lower, East and West, has been completed, and this day a new volume is opened. . . . "

121 ACCEPTANCE OF A RECOGNIZED SITUATION

Gleaner, Chatham, N.B.
Saturday, July 6, 1867

Letter from "Newcastle," dated July 4, 1867.

"[On July 1st] every one who could raise a horse was off into the country . . . . It was satisfactory to see the rigid and uncompromising Antis who always had the hardest word for Confederation, bow to the march of events and accept the 'situation' with a good grace. . . . "

122 A BIRTHDAY POEM

British Columbian, New Westminster
Tuesday, May 30, 1865

This poem has never been published. It was alleged to have appeared first in the Fredericton *New Brunswick Reporter,* composed by the conductor of the band of the 1st Battalion, 15th Regiment, and dedicated to Leonard Tilley. Here, however, it is copied from a British Columbia paper.

"Confederation Galop"

"Old Newfoundland shall stretch its hand
To young Vancouver's Island,
And all between shall hail the scene,
O'er forest, field and highland;
With banns proclaimed, and guests all named,
Through ev'ry town and station
We'll all unite in feast or fight
To hail Confederation."

Bibliographic Essay

The theme of Confederation has exercised the talent, energies, and perhaps also the patriotism of many Canadian historians, and by now, especially after the centennial of 1967, the amount of writing is considerable. Early books, like R. G. Trotter's *Canadian Federation* (**Toronto**: J. M. Dent, 1924) tended to emphasize the British role, both from the viewpoint of the Colonial Office and from that of the Grand Trunk Railway, but rather to the exclusion of British North American public opinion. This is not as unreasonable as it sounds, for the British Government played a major role in pushing Confederation through. W. M. Whitelaw, in *The Maritimes and Canada before Confederation* (Toronto: Oxford University Press, 1934) covers his field with more emphasis upon colonial opinion, and especially upon issues related to Confederation like the Intercolonial railway and Maritime union. Then in 1938-9 came the Rowell-Sirois Report (the report of the Royal Commission on Dominion-Provincial relations), with its emphasis upon financial and fiscal arrangements of Confederation and upon economic history. D. G. Creighton's excellent *British North America at Confederation* (Ottawa: The Queen's Printer, 1939), which was a study for the report, is well worth reading for its judicious grasp of the way economic and fiscal issues impinge upon politics.

Thirteen years later Professor Creighton followed this up with his *John A. Macdonald: the Young Politician* (Toronto: Macmillan, 1952) that took Macdonald's life through to 1867. This book at once swept aside all previous standards for biography in Canada. It is both an intimate portrait of Macdonald and an intensely personal evocation of the times in which Macdonald moved. It is not unfair, however, to say that it may underestimate Macdonald's scepticism about Confederation in the early years of the movement, and how unwilling he was to move until circumstances, in June, 1864, virtually forced Confederation upon him. Something of this Professor Creighton does, indeed, say; but it is said as if Macdonald were biding his time, with Confederation under his hand waiting for the right moment to bring it forward, when he would probably have preferred not to have had to bother with it at all. D. G. Kerr's *Sir Edmund Head: A Scholarly Governor* (Toronto: University of Toronto Press, 1954) is rather more old-fashioned, and covers Head's career as Lieutenant-Governor of New Brunswick (1848-54) and as Governor-in-chief of Canada (1854-61). Here, however, one has to say that a reputable historian can only go as far as the sources allow him; in the sources for *Sir Edmund Head* there is nothing like the range and the saltiness of the sources for *Macdonald*.

Professor J. M. S. Careless has done two works valuable for this period. His *Brown of The Globe*, 2 **vols.** (Toronto: Macmillan, 1959-1963) is broken at 1859-60. Careless is a different writer than Creighton. He scrutinizes his man, rather than becoming, so to speak, his *alter ego*. This gives his biography of George Brown a different tone than Creighton's *Macdonald*. Objective versus subjective is too crude an apposition to be altogether meaningful, but it does suggest roughly the kind of polarity. Careless' second work, *The Union of the Canadas, 1841-1857* (Toronto: McClelland and **Stewart**, 1967) in the Canadian Centenary Series is important for purposes of this study, especially the last chapter of the book, "The pattern of disunion, 1856-57." The difficulty with the sister book, by W. S. MacNutt, *The Atlantic Provinces, 1713-1857* (Toronto: **McClelland and Stewart, 1965**) is inherent in the title. MacNutt is forced to cover a tremendous range both in time and in the disparate politics and development of four colonies. His *New Brunswick: a history: 1784-1867* (Toronto: Macmillan, 1963) is perhaps more directly useful.

Then come the books on the Confederation period itself, that appeared in the nineteen-sixties. W. L. Morton's *The Critical Years: the Union of British North America, 1857-1873* (Toronto: McClelland and Stewart, 1964) in the Canadian Centenary Series covers the whole ground of Confederation in these years. It is based on a large amount of new research, and is really central to the theme of this book. Just putting *The Critical Years* together was a considerable achievement, for it ranges from Newfoundland to Vancouver Island. Professor Creighton's *Road to Confederation, 1863-7* (Toronto: Macmillan, 1964) is more narrow in point of time, but is a very good account of the great "take-off" of 1864 through to 1867. The present author, P. B. Waite, has published two books that can be mentioned. Though one would like to write a critical essay on one's own work in the perspective of a decade or so, let the titles suffice: *The Life and Times of Confederation, 1864-1867* (Toronto: University of Toronto Press, 1962), and *The Confederation Debates in the Province of Canada, 1865* (Toronto: McClelland and Stewart, 1963), the introduction to which may be useful.

There are useful essays in W. L. Morton, ed., *The Shield of Achilles: Aspects of Canada in the Victorian Age* (Toronto: McClelland and Stewart, 1968), notably L. S. Fallis, "The idea of progress in the Province of Canada: a study in the history of ideas," pp. 169-83; L. F. S. Upton, "The idea of Confederation 1754-1858," pp.184-207.

Extensive bibliographies of the Confederation movement are available in W. L. Morton's *The Critical Years*, and the author's *The Life and Times of Confederation*, both noted above.

Checklist of Newspapers Used in This Book.

Newspapers change, and not infrequently, in name, owners, editors, periodicity, and political allegiance. This checklist is thus tentative rather than definitive.

Name. Newspaper mastheads also change. For example, at different times the Saint John *Morning Telegraph* was the *St. John Morning Telegraph.* There was also a weekly edition of same paper called the *Weekly Telegraph.* In this book I have used and cited the masthead as it was at the time.

Dates. The dates are those that the newspaper was in existence. If it is still in existence, the original date is followed by +. Many newspapers have been amalgamated; the Saint John *Morning Telegraph* is now the Saint John *Telegraph-Journal,* as the Toronto *Globe* is now the *Globe and Mail,* a change that dates from 1936.

Periodicity. There are changes here too. The designations that are used below are only roughly correct. Abbreviations are as follows: w=weekly; sw=semi-weekly; tw=tri-weekly (a common form in Canada East and the Maritime colonies); d= daily.

Owner or editor. Owners and editors were, in important papers, often quite different. George Brown with his Toronto *Globe* is exceptional in being owner and editor of a large city daily. I have used either in the list that follows, whomever I felt, on thin evidence to be sure, to be the more significant.

Political persuasion. This too is often uncertain, and what follows is only a rough guide. In New Brunswick political labels are particularly treacherous, and this caution applies to a lesser degree in Newfoundland.

Name	Owner or Editor	Political Persuasion
CANADA WEST		
Aurora Banner, 1861 +, w	W. L. Matthews	Reform
Barrie *Northern Advance,* 1854-71, w	D. Crew	Conservative
Belleville *Hastings Chronicle,* 1841-73, w	A. Diamond	Reform
Belleville *Intelligencer,* 1834 +, w	M. Bowell	Conservative
Hamilton *Spectator,* 1846 +, d	Wm. Gillespie	Conservative
London Free Press, 1849 +, d	J. Blackburn	Reform, pro-J.S. Macdonald
Oshawa Vindicator, 1854-1917, w	S. Luke and W. Orr	Conservative
Ottawa *Citizen,* 1849 +, sw	Robt. Bell	Conservative
Perth Courier, 1834 +, w	A. L. Walker	Reform and Independent
Prescott Telegraph, 1850-97, w	P. Byrne	Reform
St. Catharines *Evening Journal,* 1835-1919, d	Wm. Grant	Reform
St. Thomas *Weekly Dispatch,* 1855-78, w	P. Burke	Conservative
Sarnia Observer, 1853-1920, w	J. R. Gemmill	Reform
Stratford Beacon, 1855 +, w	W. Buckingham	Reform
Toronto Daily Colonist, 1838-59, d	G. Sheppard	Independent Conservative
Toronto *Globe,* 1844-1936, d	G. Brown	Reform
Toronto *Leader,* 1852-78, d	J. Beaty	Conservative
CANADA EAST		
Montreal *Gazette,* 1785 +, d	B. Chamberlin	Conservative
Montreal *Herald,* 1811-1959, d	E. G. Penny	Reform-Liberal
Montreal *La Minerve,* 1826-1899, d	Duvernay Frères	Conservative
Montreal *L'Ordre,* 1858-71, tw	J. Plinguet	Liberal and Catholic
Montreal *La Patrie,* 1854-58, tw	M. A. Morel	Liberal-Conservative
Montreal *Le Pays,* 1852-71, tw	A. A. Dorion	Rouge
Montreal *Pilot,* 1844-62, d	R. Campbell	Reform
Montreal *Transcript,* 1836-65, d	D. McDonald	Independent
Montreal *True Witness,* 1850-1910, w	E. Clerk	Catholic and Independent
Quebec *Le Canadien,* 1806-91,tw	F. Evanturel	Independent
Quebec Daily News, 1862-70, d	J. Donaghue	Irish-Conservative
Quebec *Le Courrier du Canada,* 1857-1901, tw	E. Renault	Independent Conservative, and rather ultramontane
Quebec Daily Mercury, 1805-1903, d	J. Blackburn	Liberal-Reform
Quebec *Morning Chronicle,* 1847-1924, d	J. J. Foote	Conservative
NEWFOUNDLAND		
St. John's *Courier,* 1844- ?, sw	J. Woods	Pro-Confederation and Wesleyan

Name	Owner or Editor	Political Persuasion
St. John's *Day-Book*, 1862-5, d	F. Winton	Independent Conserative and anti-Confederation
St. John's *Morning Chronicle*, 1865-81, d	F. Winton	Independent Conservative and anti-Confederation
St. John's *Newfoundlander*, 1807-84, sw	E. D. Shea	Liberal, Catholic and pro-Confederation
St. John's *Patriot*, 1833-95?, w	R. H. Parsons	Liberal, anti-Confederation
St. John's *Public Ledger*, 1820-82, sw	H. Winton and Estate	Conservative and Protestant
St. John's *Times*, 1832-95, sw	J. McCoubray	Independent Conservative

PRINCE EDWARD ISLAND

Charlottetown *Examiner*, 1847-1922, w	Ed. Whelan	Liberal, Catholic and pro-Confederation
Charlottetown *Islander*, 1842-72, w	W. H. Pope	Conservative, pro-Confederation
Charlottetown *Monitor*, 1857-64, w	J. B. Cooper	Conservative, Protestant, anti-Confederation
Charlottetown *Protestant*, 1859-65, w	D. Laird	Protestant
Charlottetown *Ross's Weekly*, 1859-64, w	J. Ross	Independent
Charlottetown *Vindicator*, 1862-4, w	E. Reilly	Liberal, Catholic
Summerside *Progress*, 1866-82, w	T. Kirwan	Liberal, annexationist

NOVA SCOTIA

Halifax *Acadian Recorder*, 1813-1930, tw	H. Blackadar	Independent, anti-Confederation
Halifax *British Colonist*, 1848-74, tw	A. Grant	Conservative, pro-Confederation
Halifax *Bullfrog*, 1864-5 ?, w	J. B. Strong	Independent, anti-Confederation
Halifax Citizen, 1863-7, tw	Garvie and McDonald	Liberal, anti-Confederation
Halifax *Evening Reporter*, 1860-79, tw	J. G. Bourinot	Independent, pro-Confederation
Halifax *Morning Chronicle*, 1844-1947, d	Wm. Annand	Independent, pro-Confederation to January 1865, then anti-Confederation
Halifax *Morning Journal*, 1854-65, tw	Wm. Penny	Independent, pro-Confederation
Halifax *Sun*, 1845-67, tw	A. J. Ritchie	Liberal, anti-Confederation
Halifax *Unionist &* *Halifax Journal*, 1865-69, tw	J. McCully	Liberal, pro-Confederation -
Yarmouth Herald, 1833 +, w	A. Lawson	Conservative, anti-Confederation
Yarmouth Tribune, 1855-83, w	W. R. Huntingdon	Liberal, anti-Confederation -

NEW BRUNSWICK

Chatham *Gleaner*, 1829-80, w	J. H. Pierce	Liberal, anti-Confederation
Fredericton *Colonial Farmer*, 1863-?, w	C. S. Lugrin	pro-Tilley, pro-Confederation

Name	Owner or Editor	Political Persuasion
Fredericton *Head Quarters,* 1842-75 ?, w	J. Graham	Tory, anti-Confederation
Fredericton *New Brunswick Reporter,* 1844-1902, w	J. Hogg	pro-Tilley, pro-Confederation
Sackville *Borderer,* 1856-80, w	E. Bowes	pro-Smith, anti-Confederation
St. Andrews *Standard,* 1833-80, w	A. W. Smith	Independent
Saint John *Colonial Empire,* 1861-3, d	M. H. Perley	pro-Confederation, pro-Intercolonial
Saint John *Daily Evening Globe,* 1858-1927, d	J. V. Ellis	pro-Smith, anti-Confederation
Saint John *Morning Freeman,* 1849-84, tw	T. W. Anglin	pro-Smith, anti-Confederation
Saint John *Morning Journal,* 1865-9, tw	Wm. Elder	pro-Tilley, pro-Confederation
Saint John *Morning News,* 1839-84, tw	E. Willis	pro-Tilley, pro-Confederation
Saint John *Morning Telegraph,* 1862-1923, d	J. Livingston	Independent, pro-Confederation
Saint John *New Brunswick Courier,* 1811-65, w	T. and G. Chubb	Independent, pro-Confederation

THE WEST

Name	Owner or Editor	Political Persuasion
Winnipeg *Nor'Wester,* 1859-69, fortnightly	Wm. Coldwell and J. Ross	anti-Hudson's Bay Company, pro-Confederation
New Westminster *British Columbian,* 1861 +, sw	John Robson	Reform, pro-Confederation
Victoria *British Colonist,* 1858 +, d	A. de Cosmos	Independent, pro-Confederation
Victoria Weekly Chronicle, 1864-6, w	Higgins and Macmillan	Independent